HE CALLED ME SISTER

SUZANNE CRAIG ROBERTSON

HE CALLED ME SISTER

A TRUE STORY OF FINDING HUMANITY ON DEATH ROW

Foreword by Sister Helen Prejean,
author of *Dead Man Walking*

Preface by Bill Moyers

Morehouse Publishing
NEW YORK

Morehouse Publishing, 19 East 34th Street, New York, NY 10016

Morehouse Publishing is an imprint of Church Publishing Incorporated.

Cover photo: © Leezsnow for IStock, iStock-157193288
Cover design by Paul Soupiset

Library of Congress Cataloging-in-Publication Data

Names: Robertson, Suzanne Craig, author.
Title: He called me sister : a true story of finding humanity on death row
    / Suzanne Craig Robertson.
Description: New York, NY : Morehouse Publishing, [2023] | Includes
    bibliographical references.
Identifiers: LCCN 2022039548 (print) | LCCN 2022039549 (ebook) |
    ISBN 9781640655959 (hardback) | ISBN 9781640655966 (epub)
Subjects: LCSH: Johnson, Cecil C., 1956-2009. | Robertson, Suzanne Craig. |
    Death row inmates--Tennessee. | Friendship--Tennessee.
Classification: LCC HV8701.J64 R63 2023 (print) | LCC HV8701.J64 (ebook)
    | DDC 364.6609768--dc23/eng/20221011
LC record available at https://lccn.loc.gov/2022039548
LC ebook record available at https://lccn.loc.gov/2022039549

DEDICATION

To Cecil, who made me promise to tell his story.
We did it, my friend.

And to Alan, Anne Grace, and Allie, you are my heart.
This is our story together.

... [F]or I was hungry and you gave me food, I was thirsty and you gave me something to drink, I was a stranger and you welcomed me, I was naked and you gave me clothing, I was sick and you took care of me, I was in prison and you visited me.

Then the righteous will answer him, "Lord, when was it that we saw you hungry and gave you food, or thirsty and gave you something to drink? And when was it that we saw you a stranger and welcomed you, or naked and gave you clothing? And when was it that we saw you sick or in prison and visited you?" And the king will answer them, "Truly I tell you, just as you did it to one of the least of these brothers and sisters of mine, you did it to me."

—*Matthew 25:35–40 (NRSV)*

"I can't speak on Johnson's guilt or innocence," Denver Schimming told *The Tennessean* as he prepared protest signs for the Tennesseans for Alternatives to the Death Penalty vigil. "But the process of convicting him was fraught with problems. There was no weapon found, no physical evidence and no proceeds of the robbery found."

—*"Tennessee Executes Cecil Johnson,"* The Tennessean, *December 2, 2009*

CONTENTS

FOREWORD

I NEVER MET CECIL JOHNSON AND I DON'T KNOW IF HE WAS GUILTY of the crimes for which he was convicted and sentenced to die.

What I know is that he was a human being, a person, a child of God.

What I know—based on the words and actions of the person who my beliefs (and not incidentally, Christianity) are centered around—is how Jesus would have felt about execution, about a government deciding to end a person's life.

What I know is that getting a trial where all the angles are explored is much less likely for a poor Black man in our country.

This book by Suzanne Craig Robertson helped me get to know Cecil Johnson through his writing, her memories, and accounts of the journey that her young family took when her husband Alan signed up to visit him on Tennessee's death row. And she did not even want to do it! But eventually she did it, and like so many times we do something we don't think is right for us, it turned out to be the thing that changed her heart, her thinking, and showed their children what showing up looks like. Alan and his family *showed up*.

And through some mysterious power, these relationships that formed and tightened over fifteen years offered hope and healing, even in the face of these seemingly unchangeable circumstances. Now I'm not talking about Cecil's circumstances actually changing. You can already tell that didn't happen. But hearts, lives, and *thinking* changed.

One change that occurs when you visit someone in prison, is focus. The gift of *presence* is the best gift we have for each other. People long for people to really be present to us. Not looking over our shoulder, not texting, not thinking about the next appointment. In a prison it's so stripped down, that's all you have is each other. It's taught me, it's not just prisoners who need that. I need that, too. We all desire that. It's just the two of you facing each other. It has taught me a lot about being present. To be able to be present is the best that life gives us. Spiritual depth is about, to be able to be, present.

The book also delves into what Suzanne stumbled across way too late, that like many of the people in similar circumstances as Cecil, the playing field was a bit skewed. Through court documents and news accounts, she made some unsettling discoveries, years after his death.

There are long-known statistics that most inmates on every death row across the country are poor, Black, and often represented by lawyers with little experience in the area. If you come from a place of privilege—like I did and like the Robertson family did—you are going to be skeptical about this. But I promise you, the system is just not going to treat these people the same as white people with high-powered lawyers. It just doesn't. This was a hard pill for Suzanne to swallow, since she has worked with, and respected lawyers and the judicial system for nearly thirty-five years. But it's just a fact that prosecutors will think longer and harder before seeking the death penalty against a well-positioned and well-represented defendant, as opposed to someone in a position of vulnerability.

If truth doesn't come out at trial to exonerate, then chances are, if you don't have a good attorney, if they don't know the

law well and don't speak out—and sometimes even if you do—
you're dead.

I invite you to look into it. If you are pro–death penalty, I
know you would want it to be carried out correctly, fairly
applied, and against the right person. But in so many states, that
does not happen. For example, the American Bar Association
conducted a study that looked at ninety-three factors to ensure
that when the death penalty is applied, it is done fairly. That
should take care of it, right? But in Tennessee where Cecil was
executed, the ABA Study found that of the nearly one hundred
basic standards to ensure fairness, only seven are in place there.
Seven.

Every year, wrongfully convicted people are proven to be
mistakenly on death row. That doesn't seem like a good enough
system, especially if some of the innocents are executed. What
if it turns out to be the wrong person? (But also, what if the
person *did* commit the crime? Jesus wouldn't have been for that,
either.)

But Suzanne and Alan didn't know any of that at the time
they became friends with Cecil. They didn't know any of that
and didn't seem to believe that the State would actually kill him,
when they took their daughters to visit him on death row. Doing
this helped create a relationship that would strengthen them all
while at the same time tear their hearts out. They just went to
the prison with the idea that they were supposed to somehow
be the "hands and feet of Jesus." But you know what happened?
Like so many times, the tables flipped, and guess who ended up
feeling more ministered to?

Reading this story—about the evidence that was withheld
from Cecil's defense lawyers for so many years, that two eyewitnesses didn't pick him out of a lineup the first two times,
that his alibi witness mysteriously switched to the prosecution

in exchange for immunity the week before the trial, that there was zero physical evidence, such as a gun or money from the robbery—it's hard to imagine that the man is dead and buried, courtesy of the State of Tennessee. Nearly half of our states have abolished the death penalty, but it's alive and well down there in the South.

Who knows if Cecil Johnson was innocent or not. Now we'll never know and if we did, it is too late to do anything about it. But that's not the point anyway.

What I know is that this family showed up for Cecil Johnson and he showed up for them. They were present to each other for a long, long time. With a bond laced with sadness and joy, he and his circumstances changed the direction of their thinking. And that is something powerful.

Sister Helen Prejean
July 2022

PREFACE

FOR THE FIRST TIME IN THE FIFTEEN YEARS THAT SUZANNE CRAIG Robertson has been coming to Nashville's Riverbend Maximum Security Institution, she is here alone. She and her husband Alan have always visited together, but he is away on urgent business, and she has come on because time is short and Cecil Johnson has but a few days to live. She pauses at the entrance, then walks through a series of slow-opening gates, surrounded by loops of fourteen-foot fences topped by sharp concertina wire. Her eye catches the razor wires that slice behind the landscaping, then registers the huge, red-and-white-striped tent and the remote satellite dishes extending skyward from boxy news vans "like claws searching for prey." She moves more slowly, taking in the "beautiful, cold and clear day," wondering "if Cecil will get to see such a sight again … ," knowing it isn't likely. After she turns into the next building, a guard takes her elbow and guides her a different and unfamiliar way, not the usual route to death row. They go through a visiting room, past vending machines where she and her family had bought candy, drinks, and potato chips for Cecil over the years. She stops as she feels the first of many waves of nausea. There, she sees a door she has never noticed before. And she realizes: the death chamber is behind the snacks.

With this summation I have brought you to the lip of Suzanne Robertson's moving story of a death in Tennessee. As she lived it, so did others, and she has searched their records, accounts, and testimonies to painstakingly produce this compelling, sad, puzzling, and inspiring book. Inspiring because while the story is both disquieting and troubling, it is gracefully intimate, respectful of all parties, tender and moving. As I read, I kept thinking of the prime-time documentary I reported for CBS News in 1977 of the execution by a five-man firing squad of the convicted killer Gary Gilmore—the first execution since the Supreme Court had declared a moratorium on state killing ten years earlier. I still sense emotions I had experienced then, emotions I tried to set aside out of concern for "objectivity." But there was nothing "objective" about the way I felt interviewing Gilmore's brother as we waited for the sound of rifle fire. Occasionally I still dream from that week.

So, readers, Suzanne Craig Robertson does us a great service. She subtly honors the emotions inevitable in a story of innocence and guilt; of our collectively taking a life; of race and politics, right and wrong, and of wrestling with questions haunted by biblical memories that we confront every day, in this and every year of our Lord:

Are we not brothers?

Are you not my sister?

Are we not a family?

Bill Moyers
August 2022

PROLOGUE

A LONG WAY FROM HOME FOR ALL OF US

One by one my family members stopped coming to see me; a few of them said that I embarrassed them, and I haven't seen them anymore. As for my father, I had him removed [from my visitation list] because I couldn't stand to see him anymore. Nevertheless, I knew that I had to forgive my father for all that he had done to my life.

—Cecil Johnson, 2005[1]

EXCEPT FOR THE EXTRA GUARDS DOWN BY THE ROAD, ALL APPEARS normal as I drive up to the prison, winding through serene flowerbeds and carefully manicured edges, which do their part to hide the tension of the extra high security. The place is on lock-down as it prepares for the execution of a friend of mine.

At the top of the grand entrance of Riverbend Maximum Security Institution in Nashville, Tennessee, landscaping no longer can conceal its purpose as razor wire and featureless rectangle buildings rise in my view planted like guards themselves. I see a huge red and white tent dominating the otherwise empty visitor's parking lot. *That's new*, I think. The blank faces of remote satellite dishes extend skyward from boxy news vans like claws searching for prey.

I am at the prison for the first time without my husband, Alan. In fifteen years of visiting Cecil C. Johnson II, this is the first time I have come alone. But today is November 30, 2009, and Cecil is scheduled to be killed by lethal injection in the early morning of December 2—if no court or the governor intervenes. Alan, who works in state government, has an urgent but unrelated meeting with the governor's wife about a building project, and will visit Cecil later today. Time is short, and I had decided I better not wait for him.

When I first walk up to the processing desk, the guard assumes I am a lawyer. He starts to check me in, but when he realizes his mistake and that I am also "not family," he tells me I can't go in. I don't mean to cry. It just happens as I tell him about how I am more like family than most of the people related to him by blood. The commotion catches the attention of another guard, whom I'd seen many times out here at Riverbend. She knows my face and vouches for me, but the first guard is unmoved. The friendly guard says, "Wait here," and goes to make my case to the warden.

I study the cold government-colored block walls, the plastic bucket seats connected into rows and the oversized, dog-eared ledger where visitors sign in, and I wonder how I will get word to Cecil if they don't let me see him. After some time, the friendly guard appears around the corner from the warden's office. She's smiling, so I know that she was able to get me approved for the visit.

"You can go in until his wife gets here, in about thirty minutes," she says. I am so relieved and grateful that I leap toward her for a hug, forgetting momentarily that she's a prison guard packing heat.

She stiffens her back and barks, *"Don't do that!"*

"Oh! I'm s-s-s-sorry," I say, standing up straighter as if to show I will do whatever she says.

"I switched shifts, so I could be here today," she says in a low whisper that I can barely make out. As we walk toward the processing desk, she adds that she has always liked Cecil.

She leads me to the metal detector, stamps my hand, and frisks me as I stand without my shoes, in a private room. For the first time I am less focused on her hands sliding all over my body and more on getting inside the gates. After I put my shoes on, we head out the back door. We walk through a series of now-familiar loud, slow-opening and closing gates, surrounded by fourteen-foot double fences topped by loops of jagged and sharp concertina wire. It's a beautiful day, cold and clear, the heavens a watery blue, an irony against the bleak reason for my visit. I lift my face toward the sky and wonder if Cecil will get to see such a sight again. At the next building, we are buzzed in through a heavy door, and I hold up my hand under a black light for that guard to see my purple glowing hand stamp, which is even more important on the way out.

I take the turn inside the first building as I always have, but my guard catches my elbow and leads me a different way than toward Unit 2, death row. I don't understand at first— she is pointing me toward the vending machines of the main building's visiting room, where over the years we'd spent lots of dollars getting Chili Cheese Fritos, pecan pie, popcorn, and microwave bar-b-cue sandwiches to take into Unit 2. As we get closer, she veers to the right, and I feel the first of many waves of nausea as I realize there is a door next to the drink machine that I'd never noticed.

The death chamber is behind the snacks.

We continue past to another series of buzzing doors. I sign my name in what seems more like a guest book at a bed and breakfast rather than a log on death row. I suppress the urge to write a comment there, like, "Had a great stay!" or "Best killing facility this side of the Mississippi—good job!" Then, I am led to a tiny room that has a waist-high glass window embedded with a crisscross of wires on one wall. Through the window is another, similar room, about the size of a wide closet.

Cecil is not there yet. The guard has left me, and I try sitting in one of the plastic chairs—like you might have on your patio for a picnic—but that leaves me nose-high to the glass, so I stand. Shifting from one foot to the other, I suddenly feel awkward to be here and wonder what we're going to talk about.

I hear him before I see him.

All these years, because of his good behavior, we have visited Cecil in an open room, where we could play cards, eat together, laugh, and forget where we all were for a while. Today, I can't see his feet, but I can *hear* them. The chains, so thick you might use them to pull a car out of a ditch with a tractor, are clamped on his ankles and drag on the hard floor. He is wearing an awkward white cotton tunic and is barefoot. He tells me later they had taken his clothes and shoes, and that his feet are cold.

He backs into the little room through the glass, not looking at me, while the guard closes and locks the door. Cecil puts his shackled wrists through a narrow opening in the door, like a mail slot, while the guard unlocks the chains and pulls them off. Each link clanks on the metal door as it slithers through. He turns slowly toward me, and I catch my breath. He looks like a preacher in a baptistery, in that white tunic. Cecil spreads his arms wide and places his hands on the lower frame of the window, outstretched. My mind flies back to the many baptisms I have witnessed where the pastor stands waist-high in water, looking down onto the congregation with reassurance. There, the water laps happily onto the glass-fronted pool, and it goes something like this:

"What is your profession of faith?"
"Jesus is my lord and savior."
"I baptize you, my brother in Christ, in the name of the Father, and of the Son, and of the Holy Spirit."

When Cecil speaks, I'm jolted from that safe space of resurrection waters, back to this death chamber reception room.

"I don't know what they think I'm going to do," he says, nodding toward that door with the slot. He puts his hands up on the glass toward me. I put mine up to his on my side of the glass. I'm sobbing now and I can't breathe.

For years now, Cecil has referred to me as his little sister. Although he has many biological siblings, he told us that he felt that God had sent our family because he didn't hear from most of his own family much anymore. For the record, that's a little bit of pressure—to be *enough* to fill that role.

"I can take my daughter crying, and my wife crying," he whispers just loud enough so I can still hear him through the glass. "That just makes me stronger for them. But. Not. You. Not you." He's crying now too. It's the first time I have ever seen him cry in fifteen years. Rivulets of tears make shiny streaks on his dark cheeks.

He tells me how the guards are recording everything he says and does. He's hopeful that a stay of execution will come from the Supreme Court, Sixth Circuit Court of Appeals, or even the governor. He recounts the football game from the day before when it looked as if our hometown Tennessee Titans were going to lose, but they pull it out, beating the Arizona Cardinals with six seconds to go. Commentators called it a "legendary comeback." Cecil describes that last play in detail with a hopeful smile, comparing his situation to that one. Only the fanatical faithful believed the Titans would come out on top, down at the wire, and he's got that same against-all-odds faith today for himself.

I am not as hopeful as he is, and I don't understand football anyway. I keep both of those thoughts to myself.

He tells me how much he loves his daughter, his grandkids, his wife, Sarah, our family, and Jesus. How he isn't worried because of the promise of heaven. How either way he'll be okay.

I had thought these thirty minutes would never end, but the moments flew by.

When our time is up, we both say, "See you tomorrow." The guard escorts me out. As I pass by the snack machines, I see Sarah being escorted in. We stop for a tight hug, but because time is short and she is anxious to see Cecil, she rushes toward the door.

The guard walks me back into the bright sunshine, where I am free to go where I please. I skirt past that massive media encampment in the parking lot. *Circus tent*, I think absently, as I rush to the safety of my car, pushing down the nausea where I sit, stunned.

How did it come to this? I never even meant to get involved.

PART ONE

FAMILY

CHAPTER ONE

IT STARTED WITH A PHONE CALL ... AND POETRY

———

NO, I DID NOT MEAN TO GET INVOLVED WITH CECIL. I WAS SUPPORTIVE when Alan decided to commit to visit someone on death row. Really, I was. Supportive in that you-go-ahead-but-I-don't-want-to-get-dirty kind of way. I sat attentively listening at our church one Wednesday night while two men, the Rev. Joe Ingle and Harmon Wray from the Southern Prison Ministry,[1] explained the program that connected visitors and inmates in the name of Jesus. Not to convert anyone, not at all, but to *be* Jesus to the inmates in an unobtrusive hands-and-feet way. That means don't just sit around wringing your hands praying for someone but get in there and *do* something to help. Like Jesus did.

This concept of caring for others in the way Jesus would have was not new to me. One of the founders of the Southern Prison Ministry, the Rev. Will D. Campbell, had been a lifelong mentor to my dad on this and many other subjects. My father and my mother, in turn, had instilled in me, as if through osmosis, this concept of justice and mercy and a basic awareness of how we should help "the least of these" as Jesus had explained in Matthew 25. That Bible passage is a tough one to live by. It's all about how when you give food to the hungry or water to the thirsty, welcome a stranger, care for the sick, or visit someone in prison, well, it's as if you are doing that *for* Jesus, too. As if you should be doing these things for people all along. This was drummed into me from childhood, even though I didn't always pay attention to it.

At the other end of the spectrum, when Alan was a boy, his father had taken him to the old state penitentiary to show him "Old Sparky," Tennessee's electric chair. It was meant to be a cautionary tale, sort of a "scared straight" type of field trip. In fact, Alan would've said at the beginning of this journey with Cecil that he was a death penalty supporter. He could clearly imagine that if someone killed one of his family members, he, too, would want the murderer dead. But like so many things, once you see the details up close, know the people involved, and—in Cecil's case—see that his conviction contained many iniquities, it becomes much less of a black-and-white issue. Like, *what if you kill the wrong person?*

That night at our church, Joe had described a crime scene that resulted in the impending death sentence for a death row inmate, Phillip Workman, in such detail and passion that we could almost see it unfold before us.[2] Joe believed in Mr. Workman's innocence, but he was quick to point out to us, the potential volunteers, that not everyone on death row was innocent. That was not even the point. We were not to focus on the crime but to love the inmates in the name of Jesus, period.

Yuck. Surely, Jesus didn't mean for *me* to dirty my hands with this. It made sense on paper, like when he pointed out this type of ministry in the book of Matthew, and in Joe and Harmon's presentation, but I knew it was not for me. Seriously, that could not possibly be for me because, well, it sounded emotional, painful—and *hard.*

Before Alan met Cecil, they corresponded, talking about the subjects that had brought them together, having listed them on each of their interest forms: weightlifting, racquetball, and other sports. That they each had one daughter was a bonus.

In his first letter, Cecil described himself in beautiful, flowing cursive:

10/1/94

I'm into working out and staying in shape. I'm into writing poems. Love sports. Have a very good sense of humor, like good jokes. Most of the people who feel they know me, "thinks I'm a smartass" ☺, but I think its only the matter of opinion. I don't smoke or drink. Not into no sort of drugs. Stop smoking nearly nine years ago. I have a daughter. Her name is Deangela N. Johnson. My wife passed some years ago.

I won't bore you much more with my tedious interests and past. So I stand close for now.

Washing laundry at our house required walking down a set of steep, wooden stairs into the basement, cold in winter and cool in summer. It was also our entrance from the driveway, but the area remained dank and unlivable, except for one brightly lit corner near two of the few windows. This was our make-shift laundry room. An old black rotary phone, original to the 1950 house, hung on the wall next to the wavy-paned door to the outside. In the daytime from this spot, I could peer out into the backyard and see our golden retriever stretched in the sun, as if he were on vacation. I could leave my four-year-old daughter, Anne Grace, on the swing while I ran in to move the wet laundry from the washer to the dryer. But at night, all I could see was my own reflection silhouetted on the shiny rectangles of the blank windows.

One evening after work, I was starting a load of clothes when the phone rang. It was 1994, and if caller ID existed, we didn't yet know about it. I picked up the phone.

"You have a collect call from—" a metallic robotic voice said, then it paused long enough for a human voice to hurriedly say, "Cecil Johnson," and then the robotic voice picked back up again with, "an inmate at Riverbend Maximum Security Prison. To accept, dial one. To block inmate calls, dial nine."

By this time, Cecil and Alan had exchanged letters but had not yet met in person, so I didn't know anything about this convicted killer, except, well, that he was a convicted killer. I hadn't yet learned that as an adult with few worthy models, he had somehow pieced together his broken life and, even there in the cold hard world of prison, turned it into a work that would inspire and help others. I didn't know what he had overcome, or that his very presence in this world was a wonder. All I knew was that a jury had convicted him and sentenced him to death, and that was roughly the situation I was thinking about when I had declined to be a part of the ministry. I didn't need a picture to be able to envision his steely eyes and caustic grin. What if he asked me questions I wasn't comfortable with or said inappropriate things?

No, thank you.

I held the phone away from my ear and stared at it like it was going to bite. Alan was working late, and the call was for him, not me. I'd never talked or written to this guy. Did he even know who I was? I was home alone with Anne Grace, who was upstairs. I felt some reservation about talking to a man in prison. No, it was more than that: I got the creeps just thinking about who might be on the phone, who might be out in the backyard watching me, and who might be upstairs trying to break in the front door at that very moment. I turned toward the staring windowpane, saw my own reflection, and jumped.

There was silence on the line. I supposed he could only say his name and was cut off until I responded. I didn't know how long they would wait, but I was frozen. I wanted to dial nine, but I knew I couldn't block his calls completely, for Alan's sake. But my finger would … not … dial … one.

I hung up.

Years later when I read *Tattoos on the Heart* by Father Gregory Boyle, the image of that black rotary telephone in our basement kept popping into my head. The author describes an encounter with an alcoholic and down-trodden man he sees every day on his way to work: the man yells at him that he loves him. This surprises Boyle, and he goes to talk to the guy.

"Thank you, Junior. That was a very nice thing to say."

"Oh come on now, G, you know," he says, spinning his head in a circular motion. "You're in my … jurisdiction."

I can't be entirely sure what Junior meant. Except for the fact that we all need to see that we are in each other's "jurisdictions"—spheres of acceptance—only all the time. And yet, there are lines that get drawn, and barriers erected, meant only to exclude.

Allowing folks into my jurisdiction requires that I dismantle what I have set up to keep them out. Sometimes we strike the high moral distance of judgment—moving our protected jurisdictions far from each other.[3]

That black rotary telephone, in the basement of a house in my middle-class suburban neighborhood, was one of my ways of keeping Cecil out, keeping us out of the same community. He certainly was not in *my* jurisdiction—and I did not want to get involved, to dial 1—but I came to learn that I was in his. Cecil eventually taught me a lot, but probably more than anything over the years he taught us how to be community, how to show up, how to love someone who does not start out in your jurisdiction, is not like you. And like other great friendships, it happened while I wasn't looking.

Turns out, we are *all* in each other's jurisdictions, but I did not know that then. Cecil changed our lives, our story, by showing us that opening ourselves up to love others—who are not like us, those you might think at first who "don't deserve" it, or who are not comfortable to love—well, it can be life-changing. And not for them, but for *you*.

It took years for us to learn more about Cecil, little by little. That he was born in the rural Tennessee Maury County Hospital, in Columbia on August 29, 1956. That he lived nearby in the small town of Mount Pleasant where, he wrote, "There were only one bank, one police dept., only one stop light. ... Before schools was integrated there were two schools. Only one theatre, but I never seen it open. There wasn't any parks at the time. Most of the people were friendly; never did I encounter many times where people were prejudice toward me."

He didn't encounter "prejudice times" until he moved to the big city of Nashville. At the time, he had five sisters—Judy, Joyce, Linda, Darlene, Angela—and a brother, David. "We didn't grow up together, three of my sisters was being raised by my grandparents, my mother's parents," he wrote. Reaching way back in his memory to the beginning he remembers some happy times, though, a Christmas where his mother and father were at home, when he got the chemistry set he wanted.

"It was such a joyful time, there were so much sweets and fruits to eat." That is more in line with what Alan and I had experienced as children. We had not dug deeper into Cecil's story yet, and we did not know how "slowly it changed," as Cecil wrote. Cecil later recalled that both of his parents "started indulging frequently in alcohol. … There were many card games and such nearly ever Friday or Saturday nights. Weekends was the worse moments of my life then, for that is when my parents did there [sic] most drinking. I remember countless frightening weekend nights. … I can still hear furniture breaking, lots of loud foul language and my mom screaming as if someone was killing her."

When Alan arrived for his first visit—unaware of many details and background of this man he had agreed to see—he signed in on the huge, tattered ledger, showed his driver's license, and put his single car key in a tray, sending them along with his shoes, belt, and coat down a conveyor belt through an x-ray machine reminiscent of an airport. He took the slip of paper they gave him, with Cecil's name and number, 90996, on it. A guard motioned him to step through the tall door, which was a metal detector. A loud beep would be enough of a reason for the guard to send you back through until it could be determined that you were not trying to sneak in a knife tucked in your underwear.

Next, the guard stamped his hand. Then, there was a private room, where he was frisked by a guard, put his shoes back on, and waited for another guard to buzz open the first of many doors and gates. He was ushered outside on his way to a second building, through the confusion of fence and wire.

"There are lots of doors," Alan told me later, "but after a while you just take it for granted."

That's the truth. Cecil described taking things for granted: "Being in a place like this for twenty-three consecutive years takes away more than many would begin to realize," he later wrote. "I never thought that I would miss feeling myself walk on the grass, touching a tree, walking in the park or going outside whenever I desired to. ... I never thought that so many things that appeared so insignificant could mean so much. Things such as going to the store and choosing my own food. Taking baths instead of only a shower for years. Sleeping on a bed that don't feel like a park bench. ... Thinking about my daughter, wishing I was out to take care of her."

Walking out of the second building, Alan waited for a guard to buzz the door open after his handstamp appeared under a blacklight lamp, and he went down a sidewalk flanked by lovely shrubbery and well-trimmed grass, passing some recreational yards. These spaces were called *yards*, but they are really concrete cages with fencing on the sides and over the top; the grass stops just out of reach of the pen.

Years later, the prison would hide the yards, these cages, with privacy fences, so that visitors could walk by without ever seeing the inmates and the inmates could not see them, but on that first day, Alan walked down the path, following its sharp right and left turns to the center of a courtyard. Sidewalks crossed there, each one leading to a different building. He turned left and walked up to the door of Unit 2. He pressed another buzzer while the unseen guard inside watched him on a video monitor. A sudden loud click sounded that allowed Alan to open the door into a sallyport where the second door would not open until the outside door banged shut.

Once inside, he gave the guard his slip of paper and looked around. In front of him were three small rooms where lawyers and clients could meet in privacy. Cecil, like most of the others on death row, was able to receive visitors in the large room where several inmates and their visitors would meet at the same time.

Alan stood by the guard's desk until he was told to go in the large room and wait. And by large, I don't mean a gymnasium. More like a middle school locker room, there were plastic chairs bolted together in rows and unorganized angles. The ceiling was relatively low, about eight feet, and the walls created an oddly shaped space reminiscent of something from a geometry textbook. There was a large convex mirror right inside the door, so the guard could see all corners of the room at the same time. Alan took a seat and waited, but not for long.

"Alan?" A stocky and fit Black man a few years older than Alan came toward him. They shook hands.

"He made me feel comfortable immediately," Alan said of their first visit. "He understood how I was feeling and was sensitive to what I was experiencing, being there for the first time." Alan admitted he was a little apprehensive at first, but after a while he said he "felt more safe there than I did on the street. I wasn't afraid for my life or anything."

The two of them had a lot in common. Cecil must've been glad to be able to talk about his daughter with another dad, swap stories about how much each of them could bench press or tell a few jokes. They liked each other from the start.

Cecil called every Thursday evening to see if Alan was going to come out on Friday. Once I was used to it, I became better at dialing "1" when the robotic voice gave me the choices. At the orientation for the program, Alan had learned that it was very important not to say you're coming and then not come, so we both tried to know the answer about Friday's visit for his Thursday call. Alan had a standing Thursday racquetball game, so soon not only was he visiting Cecil on Fridays, but I began talking to Cecil on the phone on Thursdays.

Whatever Cecil and Alan had in common, Cecil and I had that same number of things NOT in common. Once we established whether Alan was going to visit the following night, I felt awkward about what to say next. That didn't last long. I soon learned that Cecil had no trouble keeping a conversation going.

"What are you cookin' for dinner?" he asked, when he heard the pots rattle and the water running.

"We're finished; I'm just cleaning up. This pot had green beans in it."

"How did you fix them?" I told him about my uncomplicated recipe relying on garlic and olive oil.

"*No ham hock*?" he said with disapproval. "Mmm, I used to put a ham hock in and let it simmer for hours."

We discussed his recipes at length—my lack of recipes, and the ingredients he used made from surprising components. He was a cook in Unit 2 and would tell me about some of the dishes he concocted. They would be based on real recipes but made with ingredients that were only vaguely similar to the original—like fried pies that used stale bread pieces instead of real dough—not only because the prison was tight on its budget, but they also didn't intend to subsidize a budding gourmet chef either. He wrote to me about how he liked to write poetry and how he first realized that after reading a poem.

For about a year [after I got to prison] I spent most of my time doing unfruitful things. That change with a request that was no more than to read someone's work: a POEM. I read it and liked it. … I was moved how he could put his feelings in words. Out of nowhere it seemed that I felt that I could do this too, that I could write like that. I tried it that very same day and the first poem I wrote were about Deangela.

I kept writing, I wrote poems nearly every day, it was like I had so much to say and no longer did I need to worry about being hurt, deceived or taken for granted when revealing my inner heart. It was a freedom I had never felt and never thought I would experience. Strangely it seemed, but I … started to learn more about myself.

[One time] a counselor … stopped at my cell, I showed him some of my poetry and he said that it was pretty good, then asked me if I had wrote any thing in prose. I told him that I didn't know what he was talking about. That is when he explained to me that I could write a poem and the words did not have to rhyme at the end of every sentence. Once I got started writing poems in prose, I soon discovered a new world, an expanded range of freedom to expound my heart. Writing became more than mere freedom, it became consoling, truly therapeutic.

Once I knew that he was a poet, a whole world of conversation opened up. *"He felt freedom when he wrote."* He started sending poems to us, and then in our weekly calls, Cecil and I talked about what inspired him to write that one, or what certain images meant, or what edits he planned to make. This poem he sent should've told me everything I needed to know about his childhood and current circumstances, but it was still early in our relationship, and I was not tuned in yet:

Here's a little story
For all the hearts that
Think they are the
Only ones who have felt
Loneliness at its full
Glory. My name is Mr.
Lonely. I have walked
On every avenue of loneliness,
And have possessed sadness
At its best. I have
Paved the streets of
Pain and been drenched
In many rains.
I've been through stormy nights,
And many plights. I
Grew up without the help
Of anyone, without any
Hand, enduring more than many
Could stand. No one
To say I love you,
When I was sad,
Down and blue. And every
Time I asked who
Am I, the answer would
Always be another lonely
Moment gone by. Many years
Have passed away and
I've watched them all day
By day. Many nights I

Have strolled a lonely
Land, and yet I
Stand tall, even though
I'm still a lonely man

Cecil began to write and write. "I felt like ever time I wrote a new poem, I freed another piece of my soul, I felt like I was liberating a part of my heart that I was convinced no one could every comprehend." Soon, he was producing booklets of poetry, which he distributed to his friends at their request. In one of his early books, he explained to readers why he wrote:

First of all, when I started writing poems, I didn't have making a book in mind. ... I now have decided to put this selection of poems out of the joy of it. And as I write them something happens within me.

I find with each poem I wrote I grew. Oh, I'm not saying that is what happens when a person writes poems. I am just relating that it is what happened to me.

Each poem is a part of the road I have journeyed and at the same time I found myself becoming a stronger man. With each poem I became more understanding about life, especially about myself.

Also I was unaware of the fact that my own faith would grow in this process at the same time. Remember as you read these poems, I didn't put them together to say to anyone how to live, they are the poems I wrote as I journeyed the roads of my life.

I wonder if Cecil realized when he began feeling the power of poetry that it would end up saving him. By expressing his feelings and faith through words, he came to terms with his life as it was, in prison, and the reality that he might die there. It did not save him physically, but mentally the act of writing helped him through every single day.

He may have had others to talk about writing, but I did not get that impression in those early years. Our phone calls remind me now of a mini writers' group, where we could focus on the words and poems and forget all else. For those thirty minutes, he was a writer, a poet, and nothing else.

Those talks probably felt like a lifeline to him, and I didn't even realize how important that was at the time.

We also talked about the weather, what Anne Grace liked to read or play, where Alan was and why he was never there when he called, how much Cecil liked to fish, when was I ever going to come visit him, and what he loved about his daughter. And soon we began to laugh. Cecil could go from serious to hysterics in two seconds, and so could I. To a fault, I often deal with tough situations through humor, and it served me well in this case. We talked and laughed as if we'd known each other for years, even though the reality of it was that this white woman and Black man likely would not have naturally found each other as friends had we not been connected through our circumstances. I found it amazingly easy to be forthright and blunt with someone who I imagined I would never actually meet in person.

We covered a lot of subjects until the robotic voice would break in and tell us that we had only two minutes left. By the time a few months of phone calls had passed, it didn't seem unusual to me that I was talking to a man in prison. In fact, often I would forget where he must be standing—surrounded by other inmates in a pod of death row—to have that conversation. He didn't dwell on where he was, preferring to talk about things that took him out of there, if only for thirty minutes. He was so good at it that I was able to go right along with him.

As normal and non-threatening as that became, talking on the phone was one thing; going to the prison was another issue entirely, and a visit was nowhere in my plans.

When Alan told me he was going to take Anne Grace to meet Cecil, I still couldn't make myself go. Alan wanted to share the happiness he felt being with his daughter because he knew Cecil would enjoy that so much, as he thought about his own daughter. Plus, Anne Grace was a lot of fun and would be a nice distraction for a person whose life was focused on the inside of a prison.

"I wasn't afraid of taking her," Alan said years later. But sitting at home that first Friday night while my whole world drove the twenty minutes to the prison *I* was afraid of, I thought, *What kind of mother lets her baby go visit someone on death row when she herself won't even go?*

CHAPTER TWO

FROM THE BACK OF THE COURTROOM

———

STREAMS OF SUNSHAFTS CUT THROUGH THE COURTROOM IN Nashville's Historic Metro Courthouse as we walked in to take our seats behind the bar. Alan had told Cecil he would be at this appellate hearing for moral support, even though there would be no contact with him. I decided that was an easy way to lay eyes on him without committing to visiting or knowing him better, so I went. My plan was: go, sit at the back, see him, leave when it was over, which would prove to him that I cared—all without having to commit or, down deep, *actually care* about Cecil. I mean, after all, the man was a vicious, convicted killer.

The first clue that my sterile plan was not going to work was when I saw a cluster of people, Black and white, sitting together, quietly looking forward with jaws clenched. I don't recall what the lawyers said or what each side was trying to prove, but as the minutes ticked away, I saw and heard the weeping, the heavy grief of the victims' family members and friends. Reliving undoubtedly the worst day of their lives, the prosecutor told his facts to persuade the judge, wounding them again with every word.

I had not counted on this. There were victims who had family who loved them.

For someone to be on death row, there has to be a victim. If the person accused did not commit the crime, there is still a victim, or victims, and there are people who loved those who were killed. In this case, as I soon found out, three people were murdered, including a twelve-year-old boy.

This situation was exactly what I had intended to avoid. Until that day, sitting in the courtroom, I had deliberately ignored the details of the crime for which Cecil had been convicted. I figured if I didn't have all that messy baggage of trying to love him while also knowing the specific sin, it would help me care about him as the Bible tells me to do. And the lawyers and judge were talking about some pretty specific sins, only a few yards away from me. The boy's close family members, including his father who had witnessed the crime, were sitting there hating the man they believed had murdered their loved ones. There was no denying the child and two men were dead. That was a fact.

I craned my neck to get a better look at Cecil. I hadn't been sure I would know who he was since I had never seen him before, but as it turned out, he was the only person in a bright orange jumpsuit with shackles and chains dragging the floor. He sat at the defense table, his back to sunny windows, his shaved head shiny. He stared straight ahead, his face stoic and angry. I wondered why he didn't try to look a little less guilty, with that grim, hardened face. He certainly did not come across as a sympathetic character.

A feeling of uneasiness came over me as I studied the people in the room, connecting who went with whom. When I got to my own bench, I realized we were tied to the least popular person in the room. Alan and I were in the courtroom to support Cecil whom we barely knew; everyone else called him a killer.

To empathize with the accused rather than the injured parties went against all my natural inclinations. If I had been dropped into this setting with no connection to it, the people I would have related to would have been those sobbing and holding their suffering hearts in their hands, not the steely-eyed man in shackles, whom I had only gotten to know through phone calls. Years later, I realized that he was hurting and injured, too, but on that day, it was not obvious.

I felt unclean and guilty, as if the family members might turn around in their pews and accuse me of *associating with* this man. I wanted to run from the room, but my immobility and need for anonymity was stronger, anchoring my heavy feet to the floor. The lawyers kept talking and talking, but I could not hear the words—it was a blessing that the spinning, white noise buzz in my head blocked images in my mind that I would not be able to erase. Images the families couldn't help but memorize. I had resisted learning specifics of the crimes and what had happened in Cecil's case to that point. All I knew was Cecil's death sentence. Now, though, the faces of family who had lost real people they loved were also part of the story.

I leaned forward a bit to get a clearer look, to study him. The table where he was sitting was perpendicular to the gallery seating. He was facing forward, which gave me and everyone else a pretty good view of him. His face gave nothing away. It didn't even look like he was registering that all the discussion was about him, but this resolute determination was probably just the way he was able to get through. Here were all these people in this room, hating him, and he knew that. I took his demeanor for shame and defiance, but later could see it as pain and distress. And anger, disbelief, and hopelessness. Once, he turned his head slowly toward the crowd, eyes searching. He paused when his gaze passed over us, and Alan gave him the slightest, almost imperceptible nod.

When we left the courtroom after the hearing, I wanted to run and run and run. This ministry was just too hard. These were families who had lost precious people on that night in 1980, fifteen years earlier—including a child, for God's sake. Who was I to be there with anything but hate and anger toward this convicted man? Wouldn't that help them more? I didn't know if Cecil had done it, and I wasn't even concerned about that. I had never even met him, nor was I listening to any evidence or lack thereof. I had been right about one thing. Knowing more was not helpful to me. If I was going to be able to "love the sinner," which I seriously doubted, details of the crime were going to have to not be part of the equation. I was not thinking of Cecil as a *person* yet and was more concerned about the effect this family friendship had on me and our family, more than what it might do for him. This was one of the lessons I learned—as well as, apparently, I am a slow learner.

The next day when the phone rang, I knew it was him. My hand crept toward the phone as I debated answering or not. Would we have to talk about what all was covered in court? Would he deny anything to me and therefore make me some kind of witness? What if he *confessed*? I picked up the phone, dreading all the weighty matters I was about to have to discuss.

"Hey, was that you?" he said.

"Where? What do you mean?"

"The one at the back of the courtroom—with the big hair?"
He was laughing hard, like my brother might have done, and
I wished he could have seen how my eyes were rolling at him.

I didn't know any more details until finally, fourteen years after
that hearing, I looked into the crimes for which Cecil had been
convicted, and also the discrepancies and the numerous legal
maneuvers that followed.

Cecil had written in his journal, sometime after that hearing,
about the first hope he felt when his appeals process got
underway, some years after he was sent to death row.

*On what seemed as a typical day, a group of lawyers came to
see me. I had no idea what for until they said that they would
like to take up my case, for they feel that I had gotten an unfair
trial. Little did I now that they was from one of if not the biggest law firm in Nashville.[1] Without knowing that, I agree to
allow them to help me. I thought finally someone else believes
I'm innocent too. That was a big relief to me and I shared with
them all that I could.*

Jim Thomas was pretty fresh out of law school, working as an
associate at Neal & Harwell in Nashville, when a senior partner,
Jim Sanders, first asked him to help represent a man in a post-
conviction capital case. They were "troubled by the fact that it
went to trial so fast," Thomas says, pointing out that the crime
was in July 1980, and it went to trial in January 1981. "Even back
then, for a capital case, that is an almost unbelievably fast track.
We didn't understand why there hadn't been a motion for a
continuance made. Nowadays for a felony case in a Davidson

County criminal trial that would be unusual—you'd expect it to be at least two or three years [before the trial]."

He says they wanted to take Cecil's case because they "felt very strongly that Cecil had not received a fair trial."

Cecil had been convicted by a Davidson County jury of three counts of first-degree murder for the murders of a twelve-year-old boy and two adult men, as well as two counts of assault with intent to commit first-degree murder for two men who survived, and two counts of armed robbery. He was sentenced to death for the murders and four consecutive life terms for the remaining convictions. His trial lawyer was Mike Engle of Nashville.

While digging up that information, I stumbled upon documents that showed that the month before the 1995 appearance in the court hearing we attended, Cecil had been convicted along with another man in the beating death of a fellow inmate at Nashville's old state penitentiary known as "the Walls." The victim was on death row for the murders of a prostitute, a Memphis policeman, and a Roman Catholic priest. I was reminded again of the good advice Joe and Harmon gave at the outset, which was to not get involved in the inmate's case. If I had known about this jailhouse murder, would I have continued on the journey?

I don't know.

Nearly two decades after that hearing, in an old manila envelope full of memories I came across a faded form from the Department of Correction, Division of Adult Institutions. Cecil's now-familiar typewriter had filled in the blanks to request a "special visit" from me for December 23, 1995—a little more than a year after Alan's first visit, and just a month or so after he laughed at my big hair at the back of the hearing.

Next to my name, birth date, address, and phone number, it said "FRIEND." The type was so faded that I could barely read the lines for "Reason for Special Visit." Still, I made it out: "Mr. Robertson is on my visitor list but his wife is not and he ask me if she could come with him … this is only for one time until I can have her placed on my visiting list." (I consider that sentence a moment, and I know in my heart that I had no intention of being placed on the regular visiting list, when I first read the request in 1995.) Below were two spaces: Recommended and Not Recommended.

The Unit Manager signed it, checked "Recommended," and wrote, "As per holiday visiting schedule." Below in a space for "Approved," the Associate Warden of Operations checked and signed it.

It was official. I was going to visit a convicted killer on death row.

CHAPTER THREE

DADDIES AND DAUGHTERS ...
AND A PERSONAL SHOPPER

AT FOUR YEARS OLD, ANNE GRACE LOVED DRESSES THAT TWIRLED.
In fact, she would not wear one if it did not fling high enough
when she went into a spin. Her long curly hair would flail out par-
allel to the skirt and the floor, her heel turning her like a top. Her
collection of baby dolls and stuffed animals was large and diverse,
and she could tell you not only their names but who gave them to
her and for what occasion. She would load them up in her white
wicker stroller to take them out for tea parties in the yard.

In her life, she had two married parents, four married grandparents, a cat, a dog, some horses, and a host of others who
loved her in her world of home, church, daycare, and happiness.
Maybe these are the reasons why going to the prison wasn't
unusual or upsetting; her daddy took her, so it must have been
okay. She recalls those early visits with a sharp eye.

"I remember walking into the lobby," she said later, at twenty-three. "Daddy was getting money for the machine, before we went to security." Nothing but a key, an ID, and a special debit card could be taken inside the prison. A rectangular, metal machine put money on the card, which was the only way to buy snacks for the inmates. They couldn't buy their own snacks, so it was important not to show up empty-handed. The money machine was near the guard station, in a side room lined with lockers where things could be stored during a visit.

"They all knew Dad, and they would talk to us," Anne Grace said. "I remember two guards there, and a book to sign, like a guest book. We walked through the metal detector." Then, she put her arm up to the counter for the guard to stamp her hand. "I took my shoes off and went in a separate room with the lady. The lady wanded me down."

This is what happened to every visitor. The small rooms to the left of the end of the conveyor belt seemed to double as storage, with shelves stacked with random supplies. Sometimes a female guard was not on duty, and there was a bit of a wait to find one to conduct the pat down. My little Anne Grace followed the guard out of the private room, got her light-up tennis shoes from the conveyor belt, sat on the nearby bench with her feet dangling, and put her shoes on. Alan was doing the same and when they were ready, he nodded to the guard, who clicked open the door to the outside.

"Sometimes I could see the sun going down," Anne Grace said. "The rest of the time it was dark." Going inside the next building, they held their hands high to the black light behind thick glass where the guard was. In those days, Alan held Anne Grace up, so her hand could reach the light. The last time she went she was tall enough to reach it herself. "I always liked having that stamp and getting to put it under the light." Then, they went into a large room, usually full of small groups of people sitting in the rows of chairs. A guard on an elevated platform stood watch over the wives, girlfriends, mothers, sons, and daughters of these inmates. This, just a detour on the way to Cecil, was a lower security area.

"I remember it was quiet in there, never loud," she said of the low buzz created by the inmates and loved ones catching up on the news, telling their daddies about school, how Grandpa was doing after surgery, that sort of thing. The room was filled with people of many races—the inmates and their families, as well as the guards. As they made their way around the edge of the room, Anne Grace held the hand of one of the few daddies who would walk out the door that day.

As adults, we'd already learned to avert our eyes, but she was taking it all in, looking into the eyes of anyone who noticed her. At the far end of the room, a line of vending machines stood with their backs to a long wall. Inmates and visitors mingled there, using their debit cards for sandwiches, candy bars, soft drinks, juice, popcorn, and pies.

"There was always that weird one, with sandwich halves and biscuits," Anne Grace recalled of a tall glass-front kiosk that rotated inside where they could pull back a small sliding door for each item, reach in, and take it out. They loaded up with Cecil's favorites and walked back through the vast visiting room, teeming with distressed people. Alan and Anne Grace left the crowded room and went out another door to the bright sunshine, walking past where inmates often would yell at visitors.

Many years later, the prison's chaplain, Jeannie Alexander, described that walk to a group of visitors: "It's not a PG-13 environment. Don't look at the windows, or you may get mooned."

Alan reports that no one yelled at them (or mooned them, for that matter), when he had young Anne Grace with him.

When they got to Unit 2, Cecil was waiting with a big grin on his face. Anne Grace stood shyly by Alan's leg, peering out at the laughing man they had come to see. If she had any thoughts about what a man in prison might be like, this happy man was not what she would've expected. Cecil popped the popcorn in the microwave while he and Alan talked, and Anne Grace looked over the books and games on a nearby bookshelf. It was a small gesture for the prison to provide such things, but for families with children visiting it made it a little more normal, slightly masking the cold, hardness of the place. They settled into a corner, and Cecil began asking questions. He was such a good listener, looking her right in the eye as she spoke to him.

"What did you do today," he asked. "What's your mom doing? How's your dog? Did you take him for a walk? Why are you so silly?" She would answer and laugh and ask him why he was so short (he was much taller than she was, of course), but it made him laugh, so she said it over and over.

"Did you used to have any pets?" she asked.

"You ask a lot of questions," he answered. "You remind me of another little girl I know." He looked at her with such deepness, his eyes were a mixture of joy and sadness.

"Who?"

"My little girl, Deangela! She's older than you though, but I remember when she was a little stinker just like you." One time when Alan was visiting the prison, Deangela, a teenager at the time, was there, and he got to meet her. Cecil was as proud as any dad ever had been. Back then, we didn't know much about them or what they had been through.

But I had only heard these early reports second-hand, because I had not yet been able to make myself go to the prison.

Other than the possible lapse in judgment of sending my daughter to death row visitation at such a young age, I was relatively ordinary for a white, middle-class, suburban working mother. Three days a week Anne Grace went to preschool while I worked as editor of a statewide legal magazine; the other days were spent playing with friends, cooking together, swinging at the park, visiting grandparents, or being at our nearby church just about every time the doors were open.

This business of going to a maximum-security prison didn't match up, but with the completed Special Visit form turned in, Alan, Anne Grace, and I headed to the prison two days before Christmas, where my five-year-old knew more about it than I did.

"Walk through this thing, Mom," she said. "And then you take your shoes off! And then, you see that door there? They'll click it real loud, and we go down there where that purple light is."

After going through the process, we were finally face-to-face with Cecil. Others were in the visiting room, and Alan made his way around, shaking hands, saying "How ya doin" to everyone, and settling in. The inmates and their visitors shook his hand or nodded to him and smiled in recognition to Anne Grace, who seemed to be among old friends. She made her way to the bookshelf of toys, picked one out, and settled onto a chair. Cecil's eyes were wide and glistening, his smile broad, and arms outstretched ready for a hug.

"Well, well, well, look who is finally here," he said to me. "I didn't think you'd go through with it."

Frankly, I had not thought I would do it either, but simply said, "Well, here I am."

Anne Grace was six when we welcomed another beautiful daughter, Allie, into our family. When she was still an infant—and

I knew this was coming—Alan told me he wanted to take Allie to see Cecil. Of course, Cecil had been asking on every phone call since her birth about us bringing her. To be able to see and hold an infant was one of the great joys of his life—because it took him back to that very short time with Deangela. This was not something I fully realized at the time, but my tender-hearted husband must have.

Years later, we learned that Cecil had not had much time with Deangela. She was about a year and a half old when he went to prison, but he had seen her over the years as she grew. He had a few in-person images of his daughter, seared into his memory, which like his own childhood memories eventually crashed out of control from happiness to despair. He recalled first peering into the hospital room where his wife, Marion, was holding their baby. Marion saw how happy Cecil was, and she started to cry, which caused him to cry, too.

"I kneel down along side of the bed and hugged her as I looked at our little girl," he wrote. When he held her for the first time, he "stared at her beautiful tenderness. I gently touched her angel soft hair, her little, tiny hands. She was so small, and I had to be very careful how I held her little head. … I felt so proud."

As their baby grew, Cecil and Marion began to navigate what it meant to be a family, what it meant to him to be a father, to provide. "Everything for us was coming along well," he wrote, as they had decided to save enough money to move out of the government housing projects where they were living.

"I will never forget how Deangela would smile, and each time it would light up my heart." As it happened over and over in his life, this bliss was not to last. "Marion was two hours late from work and I had to go to work that evening," Cecil recalled. "So I called her job, they told me that she had left a few hours ago. My first thought was that maybe she stopped to shop for something.

… Just as I was about to call her mother, to see if she would baby sit because I would have to go to work, Marion started coming through the door. So in a calm manor, I asked her where she had been, she said that she had to work overtime."

Cecil knew then she was lying and asked her several more times before, he wrote that "she broke down and told me that she had had an affair with one of her coworkers." Cecil was so angry he smashed the coffee table with his fist, saying he didn't want to hear any more. He called Marion's mother to come over. When she arrived, she saw Marion sitting on the sofa crying.

"I took Deangela and left," he said. "I got a room in a bordering house and [the lady who owned the house] agreed to baby sit for a small fee while I was at work. I will never ever forget that first night. I had only one bed, so I put Deangela on one side and I lain on the other side. I couldn't sleep, I only stared into the darkness of the room and it was so quiet that I could hear my tears as each one hit my pillow. … It was only when Deangela needed her bottle that I came out of my trance of sorrow." That night he made up his mind "to spend my life taking care of my daughter, that is how I pull myself up out of my pain." He gently carried this memory of his baby lying next to him, this pure moment of love that he treasured, for the rest of his life.

One weekend the lady who was keeping Deangela had to leave, and Cecil needed a babysitter, so he took her to his father's girlfriend's home. She had told him she would keep the baby sometime.

"After work I went to pick my daughter up and when I arrived there, Deangela was gone," he wrote. "My father had came and gave Deangela back to Marion." Cecil was so upset he didn't go back to work the next day or even the day after. "My heart was completely dark. I stayed away from my father then because I would have hurt him."

After that, Cecil got a new job at Vanderbilt University Medical Center, and he moved downtown to the Sam Davis Hotel, a once-regal building that had fallen into disrepair. It was torn down to make room for the city's new convention center a few years after Cecil lived there. The twelve-story building, built in 1928 and named for "the boy hero of the Confederacy," was one of the last fully residential boarding hotels in the city.

"My room was ten floors up," he wrote. "I could look out my window at night, and I had never envision such a captivating sight, the sight of the city looked like Christmas time every night." The first few nights especially, he "spent hours looking out the window, it was so surreal and strangely peaceful, like I was looking down on the entire world." Things were going well with his new job. "I was meeting new people, I was making the best of what I had, creating friendships at work with some good people." But he carried the sadness of missing his daughter with him always.

I finally agreed for Allie to be taken to the prison for a visit, hesitant not for Cecil to see her but for the process of getting her in to where he was. I had not been to see him since long before Allie's birth, and once the visit was set, I certainly did not want to miss seeing that introduction. Like any mother, it felt like it was a big deal for anyone else to hold my infant—I didn't hand her off to just anyone in those days, but I felt strangely confident about taking Allie to visit Cecil. It is worth noting that a baby going into the prison doesn't get much special treatment—when Allie was there, the female officer was still called in. We went in the private room, and I was instructed to take her diaper off, so the guard could inspect inside.

When Alan handed our baby to Cecil, it was clear it had been worth the effort, as he looked deep into her eyes. He was as gentle as if he were holding a fragile china teacup. His grin broke open, and he did not stop smiling the whole time. Allie soon fell asleep, not knowing someone's eyes were so close to hers, following her every breath. When she squirmed to get a better position, he would settle her back into the crook of his arm, adjusting the blanket around her. His knee jiggled slowly, keeping her in a deep sleep, until she finally reached up with her little fists and rubbed her eyes. She began to stretch and stretch, eyes blinking open in a most relaxed wake-up. When her eyes stayed open and she was fully awake, she focused on Cecil's face with curiosity. He began to talk to her as I imagine he had talked to Deangela during the limited time he had with her as a baby. He was transfixed and transported.

I don't think he looked up at the rest of us but a few times during the entire hour. We didn't have as much normal conversation that time because his main visitor was right in front of him, in his arms. He could not stop looking into Allie's eyes and touching her soft hair.

That evening was one of the best gifts I've ever helped give to anyone.

One afternoon after unloading the groceries and hauling them, bag by bag, up our steep basement stairs from the driveway in back, I headed out the front door to the mailbox.

I stood near the road, sifting through bills and junk, when a No. 10 white envelope caught my eye. My name and address were typed—not in a standardized computer print, but with a cursive typewriter that had printed some letters dark, some faded. A pale gray sentence that looked like it was the last one stamped before the guard re-inked, was on the back: "The Department of Corrections/RMSI Has Neither Inspected Nor Censored and is Not Responsible for the Contents."

I hurried back down the walk to the house because it was cold November. Inside, I dropped the stack of mail on the dining room table and began to fix dinner. I checked on Anne Grace, who was riding her spring horse so fast its front end lifted up and banged on the hardwood floor with every stride.

The unopened letter didn't haunt me, exactly. I would get to it. When I did, I found a note from Cecil asking if Alan and I would mind getting the items for his "Christmas box" this year. Whoever had done it in the past, if anyone, was unable to do it this time. I was skeptical as I studied the list. *Surely one of his sisters or his father could do this*, I thought. *You mean to tell me that I am at the front of this line?*

The list was odd and depressing to me, as it was the best he would get all year: one handball glove, t-shirts with just the right type of neck, underwear, slippers, note pads without staples, chili-cheese Fritos, and a frozen Sara Lee Cherry Cheesecake. Huh? A cheesecake? Next time he called he asked if I had gotten the list.

"Yeah, I got it," I said.

"Well? Can you do it?" By this time, Alan and I had already discussed it, him more on board than me, but we said we'd do it.

"Weird list, you got there," I told him.

"Yeah, well, they are pretty strict."

"You are kidding about the cheesecake, I guess?" I was sorry the second I said it, and there was silence on the line.

"It's my favorite, and I really miss it," he said. "If you freeze it real hard right before you mail it, it will still be okay when I get it."

"But where do you keep it? You don't have a refrigerator, do you?" His laugh was so loud that the other inmates on the pod probably turned their heads to look at him.

"Keep it? There's no keepin' it. Do you think I have a two-bedroom apartment with a full kitchen in here or something?! I eat it all at once, right when they deliver the box." This endeared him to me and saddened me at the same time. We would have a buffet full of desserts at our holiday celebration, taken for granted. The presents around our tree probably would extend so far that we would barely have room to sit. But this small box of necessities and the one cheesecake extravagance were every-thing to him.

The box had to be received during a very narrow window of time, or it would be rejected. So, with Sarah Lee Cherry Cheesecake and t-shirts with exactly the right neckline on my mind, I began.

"I got the box," Cecil later told me on the phone.

"How was the cheesecake," I asked.

"Mushy, but great!" he said. "And thanks for the extra paper—I was running out. Weird color, though, but I'll get used to it."

"You know I am rolling my eyes right now, don't you?"

Once we became the Official Shoppers for the Christmas Box, Cecil sent more requests for other approved items. The most unusual one we got was for eyeglasses, with very partic-ular color and shape specifications, which was a daunting task.

Arriving at the eyeglass store, the walls of frames towered over me as I searched for that specific pair. I wear glasses and had shopped for them many times, but what I had not done was shop for someone else—someone who was not there with me. And then, there was the added twist of *why* the person wasn't there.

"You may want to look over on this other wall," the saleslady said to me. "These here are men's frames."

"Uh, right. Actually, I am looking for men's glasses."

"Oh? Well, that *might* work for you ..."

"No, they're not for me," I said, wondering how I would put this. "They're for a friend. And I know exactly what they need to look like."

"Oh, okay. But he'll need to come try them on, so I can get exact measurements."

"Uh, yeah, of course," I said, stalling for time. I headed to the clunky plastic black frames and had to smile because he had sent a picture of frames that reminded me of Roy Orbison. In the letter with the picture ripped from a catalog, he was most excited that he was going to add a pale blue tint to the lenses. Not like sunglasses, but just a wash of light color. I had tried to talk him out of that on our next phone call, but he would not be swayed.

"I'll be the only one with glasses like this!" he had said.

"Oh yes, there's no question about that," I laughed.

Standing in the store, hesitating in front of the Roy Orbison glasses, I took a deep breath and did what I had to do. Like ripping a bandage off fast, I blurted to the clerk that "I want these frames with pale blue lenses; here's the prescription, and, and oh, by the way, the customer will not be coming in for a fitting because he is in prison." I said it—although I may have *possibly* left out the part about death row. Okay, I did leave it out. Even after all this time, I was hesitant to share my connections; I am not proud of that. From most people I had found the judgment to be strong, and it felt unnerving to know I would probably have to defend myself. There was a stigma and fear associated with my friendship with a convicted killer, one I still feel as I write these words.

It's possible that everywhere else the opinion about a death row prisoner is not the same, but in our corner of the South, I have learned to assume that people are going to be disgusted by these inmates and anyone associated with them. So, I tread lightly, not giving away my thoughts on capital punishment early in a conversation. I learned to do this mostly from being a Southern Baptist for so long, I'm sad to report.

The eyeglass clerk's pen hovered in mid-air over the form, frozen, as her face registered it all. It could go either way, I realized, and looked her in the eyes to see what she was made of.

"Well … a person really needs to be here so the fit will be right," she said. "The corporate office usually requires the customer to actually be here, but—" At the first inkling of compassion, I couldn't stop myself before I told her about my friend whom my family visits and how he needs glasses. I don't know how else to get them to him, and no, he will not be getting out any time soon.

She softened. "That's a nice thing you're doing," she said as she began to fill out the paperwork.

"You too," I said back to her.

As years passed—as governors, wardens, and related rules changed—the prison instructed us about new, more tedious rules for the Christmas boxes and other formerly approved packages, until "personal boxes" were not allowed at all. Instead, inmates were given a list of items provided by one approved company where they could order. Cecil marked the items that he wanted and sent the order form to us. We wrote a check and sent it in, but it was less personal. I was surprised to find I missed the scavenger hunt every December. He must have missed feeling loved, knowing each present or item was hand-picked by us.

Always appreciative, Cecil would call every year as soon as he received the box to thank us. Getting individually selected gifts showed him that he was cared for, that we thought about him in the process, that we knew him well enough to find just the right thing, even if was from a tightly restricted list.

After it became standardized, I felt sad that we could not give personal gifts anymore, and no more weird-colored paper. He had always made jewelry or art designed especially for each of us from prison-issued art supplies and sent them in plenty of time to sit under our Christmas tree.

The items we bought off the standardized form and had delivered to him were still useful, if overly regulated and impersonal, but the Sara Lee Cherry Cheesecake was the biggest casualty. You can bet nothing like that was on the government's list; once that became the rule, he never got to eat another one.

CHAPTER FOUR

HIS OWN SAFETY NET

———

BESIDES THE TELEPHONE AND VISITS, THE PLACE I INTERACTED with Cecil most was at the mailbox. He wrote a lot of letters. Eventually, I was glad to see that faded cursive typewriter address on the envelope. There was often a twinge of guilt when I realized how many letters he had sent since the last one we had mailed to him. The day I found a brown 9 x 12 envelope with curled up edges from being crammed in our mailbox was different.

That's weird, I thought, seeing that the envelope was from Cecil with the familiar prison disclaimer stamped on the back. Then, I remembered. Inside was his memoir, which he had asked me to read and find a publisher for. I had not been encouraging when he had asked me on the phone, telling him I did not have time to take that on. It was the truth: juggling two kids and a job kept me busy. I did not tell him the rest of the reason, which was that I didn't think there was a market for his story. Also, and not to my credit, I did not want to mire myself in his awful subject. If I were going to work on any book, it would likely not be the life story of a man on death row. (Years later, I read that last sentence and smiled, knowing that Cecil has finally gotten the last word. The idea of pursuing this story has been relentless, for reasons I cannot explain. Cecil was persistent in writing his story, and, although it took me too long to see it through, so was I.)

I pictured him pulling pages out of his old typewriter, one at a time. Everyone in the free world was already using computers, making fast typing mistakes, hitting delete, and zipping forward again. For Cecil, whose typewriter ribbon was about shot, every stroke mattered. In the early years of his incarceration, he was given a typewriter, but at some point, the prison would no longer let him receive the ribbon cartridges it needed. He was judicious and slow with his typing, and the words faded more with every reuse.

The sheets, more than fifty pages of single-spaced text, had margins less than an eighth of an inch from the edges. No white space was wasted. He then had gone back with a blue pen and marked corrections, adding a comma here, a date there. He wanted this work to be perfect, and he wrestled with every detail.

Ten years after I first met the man, I sat down in my comfortable den in a relatively privileged area of the city and made myself read his memoir. As I began to learn more, I was struck by how I could have known him so long without wondering about his backstory or seen this childhood pain in his eyes. In the background, I heard my daughters in their after-school routine of homework, laughter, and minor sibling squabbles, but that all faded as I was drawn into Cecil's early life. There could not have been more contrast between what Cecil dealt with as a child and what I had been given, which only continued into our present circumstances.

I had done nothing to deserve what I was born into, and neither had he. With every sentence where he plotted his meager life story, my mind shot to my own circumstances, and I was ashamed that I had not realized sooner how vast the differences were. Cecil's descriptions of his life were graphic and riveting. In disbelief, I could not stop reading:

His mother was screaming again, he wrote. He, and his brother and sisters, could hear furniture breaking and their father's cussing as they tried to sleep. When it got quiet, he was even more afraid because then he wasn't sure if she was still alive. He didn't slip out of bed to check on her though, not wanting a beating himself. The next day, as always after one of these nights, his mother wore her sunglasses in the house. But they couldn't hide the bruises on her arms and face, and by eight years old, Cecil had learned to go outside without question when she told him, through tears, to stop staring and go play.

One morning like that, he woke up to find that his mother was gone. She came back later that day. As she packed up her clothes, he held on to her.

"Mama, don't leave us," he cried.

"Get your hands off of me," she told him. "I wish you were dead." Cecil carried that inside him a long time and didn't forget it because his father reminded him of it a lot. Although later in his life, Cecil forgave them; at that time he was a lonely little boy whose parents had told him they didn't want or love him.

Is that something anyone ever gets over?

As I read, I kept having flashes of my own childhood—although the two journeys could not really be called by the same name because they were so drastically different.

Cecil's father stayed with Cecil and his brother, and there were some good times, although his father gambled often. There were times when he had the boys go out and dig up fishing worms, and the three of them would fish, catching enough for their dinners.

"He would drive on the back roads back home," Cecil wrote, "at the time neither David or I had any idea why. My father would stop the car, go in the trunk and grab some large burlap bags, then he came to me and said, 'Bud, slowly drive the car down the road' to a certain point. I didn't know how to drive then, but I could do that. Just as I arrived at the spot he had shown me, my father would jump out from the bushes with those burlap bags full of corn and turnip greens. He would hurry to the car and we would leave very fast. … We didn't think anything of this, plus we were too afraid of our father to question him about it, and because we were very hungry too. Oh what a meal it would turn out to be, for my father really had skills to cook."

The times the boys had with their father also included hunting, but in a rather unorthodox way. Cecil remembers being in the car as his father drove onto the nearby high school football field. Then he told Cecil to drive the car around in the field slowly.

"As I did, he would sit up on the front of the car with his shotgun and shoot rabbits," he wrote. "After he had killed about five or six of them, we would go back home and clean them, a very gruesome scene. After he would skin and gut them, he hand them to me to wash and get all the buck-shots out of them. I didn't think about how they looked or felt, I simply did what my father asked me to do."

These times when it was the three of them were difficult—many times they had nothing but grits to eat—but the boys had their father, and that counted for a lot.

One time, a teenage relative was in the house alone with him. "He wanted to come in and help me take a bath," Cecil wrote. "I kept telling him I can take a bath by myself, still he kept reaching for me, up until I told him if he didn't leave, I would tell my father." In retrospect, I wondered if what Cecil was insinuating was true and if anything would have been done had he, indeed, told his father.

Cecil's stories were alarming, and I didn't know what to think. Such as the time when Cecil wrote about his father holding him by the wrist, dragging him toward the stove. "I'm going to teach you to not play with fire anymore," his father told him. Cecil pulled back, but his father's grip held his hand above the red-hot coil. Screaming and crying, Cecil made one more effort and yanked free, running out of the house. His father called and called for him through the night, but the boy did not come back in.

Some years later, his father remarried, and with a new baby on the way, took a job in Nashville, about an hour from their home in tiny Mount Pleasant. He came home only on the weekends, which left any parenting to his new wife. Cecil claimed she would force the kids to attend to church, or risk punishment. "That's when I started running away from home," he wrote.

Then, Cecil's mama showed up. Not to ask for forgiveness or to give him a life he wished for; she came to get his sisters. She took her daughters to live with her but left her sons. Her words of wishing he was dead must've again rung in his ears that day.

My mother never said anything like that to me. Reading Cecil's devastating stories, I considered the grown man I knew and could not figure out how a person survives a childhood like that.

Cecil did have some adults in his life who loved him, but it doesn't seem like it was ever enough. "I loved being around my grandmother," he wrote. "She had very high rose cheek bones, and even when she wasn't smiling, she still had a joyful expression on her face."

It seemed like the adults in Cecil's young life were stepping up and disappointing him, one by one. Maybe they were unaware of his circumstances, but even the ones who did love him, just weren't able to muster the courage or perhaps weren't in a position to save him or his brother.

He wrote that one summer day he was at his grandmother's house, playing outside when he noticed that all the storm windows weren't all the way in, so he worked on each one so they were in correctly.

"My grandmother came outside and asked if I had put them in. I was almost afraid to answer because I thought that I was in some sort of trouble," he continued. "I was completely wrong, for she said to me that my grandfather could never get them in, and he were a carpenter. She looked down at me with a smile that truly melted my heart and said this to me: 'Sweetheart there is something very special about you.' That is something I will never ever forget." For a while, he believed her.

When he was eleven, he wrote that she sent him over to help a neighbor mow the grass and chop some wood. Sweaty and tired, the jobs done, the woman invited him in for cookies. Cecil claimed he went through her bedroom to the bathroom to wash his hands and when he came out, she sexually assaulted him.

He was learning that there were no adults he could fully trust—like his father, when Cecil was twelve, and they were in the car. It veered off the road, his father drunk, Cecil screaming "Daddy, wake up!" Cecil wrote about grabbing the steering wheel and the car jerking back between the yellow lines. Cecil rolled the window down to let in the freezing wind. Soon after, his father taught him to drive, but told Cecil to put him back in the driver's seat before they got to the edge of town.

As a child, I never once had to act as the parent in my family.

During that time, Cecil's father was still living and working in Nashville. His wife was back in Mount Pleasant with Cecil and David, but when she moved out, the boys stayed in the house, on their own. Cecil was the oldest, at thirteen.

"We still tried to go to school, but only when we wanted to," he wrote. Their father intermittently gave the boys money for food. When the money ran low, they would often be down to toasted bread with sugar on it, or grits. "Me and David started doing all we could to survive. We cut wood for people, we even stole food to eat." They raided fruit trees, and sometimes, they went to the grocery store when it was crowded, so they could eat the fruit unnoticed. "It seemed like I stayed hungry."

One of those days hanging around in a store, Cecil decided he wasn't going to miss out anymore. Standing alone in the candy aisle, he turned his head both ways, and when he thought no one was looking, he slid a candy bar into his pocket. But on his way out the door, an employee collared him. He explained, "I was so afraid; the lady let me go but ban me from the store. But it was a different story with David, oh my, he was so good. David once stole us a pair of shoes and few other things. David only done it that one time, for some reason he simply stopped."

For everyone, parts of our childhoods stand out and stay with us. Cecil wrote,

I remember one holiday so clearly. We didn't have much at all, no coats or hats, gloves and only one pair of shoes and they was so bad that we put cardboard paper in them to cover the holes. On that Christmas morning, David and I got up and put on three to four shirts, a few pair of pants and socks on our hands

for gloves, for it had been snowing for days and it was extremely
cold and messy outside. As we walked over to our grandmother
house, I remember looking at all the pretty decorations we
passed. I could hear music and laughter all around. New bicy-
cles on some of the porches. I will never forget the sadness I felt
that day. When I finally reached my grandmother's house, my
feet would be soaking wet and cold. I would park myself behind
the old wood burning stove. I remember my grandmother always
telling me to get my cold feet very close to the stove. I just loved
seeing my grandmother. She came to mean so much to me.

As I write this part of the book, I am now a grandmother myself and unable to imagine the circumstances of this woman who undoubtedly loved these boys. Did she not know their parents were gone, and there was no heat or much food in the house? If this were truly the case, I wonder why his grandmother didn't step in to help. I don't judge her because I don't know all the facts; but while reading these accounts, I wondered how many opportunities there may have been to intervene.

"Everyone in my family knew that David and I lived on our own and no one ever said a word about it, neither did we," Cecil wrote. It may have seemed normal to Cecil at the time, but later he probably saw how the adults in his life let him down once again.

On some weekends, their father would come home, which sounds like it would've been a good thing, but often that made it worse. Cecil recalls one of those visits when his father was "supposedly punishing" him.

He went beyond the normal and he kept beating me and
beating me. My pain had reached a point where I couldn't
bare it any longer, my father lost it and soon I started seeing
flashes of light, I wanted to go and die, so I started shouting

at my father to go on and KILL ME! KILL ME! KILL ME!
I don't remember when he stopped. … After that day my
father never whips me again, but still I never felt the same
about my father.

It would be years before Cecil realized the direct effect that his
father's treatment had on him, and on down the line to David.
"I did David wrong, for every time he did something I felt was
wrong, on several occasions I beat him badly. … I didn't know
that what I was doing to him was the results what my father
had done to me." Eventually Cecil stopped doing that, and the
brothers got along together again. "I realized that we only had
each other. I found it so hard trusting people anymore. Except
for David, I often felt completely all alone. I always yearned for
the type of homes and family life I saw the other kids have.
Countless times I remember looking in store windows wishing
I had some of the clothes I saw other kids wearing."

Cecil eventually got a job at a small grocery store, making
sixty cents an hour. The water and light bill were about fifteen
dollars, and rent where he and David were living was twenty-
five dollars a month. "Before my first paycheck I went window
shopping nearly every day. I wished for a new bicycle, all sorts
of foods and clothes that I was going to get when I got paid.
I worked very hard every day, finally payday was at hand. My
first payday and I couldn't wait to get to work. I was extremely
happy that morning I worked harder than ever, time seen to
move slower and slower."

At noon, a voice came over the crackly loudspeaker in the
grocery store, saying "Cecil Johnson, come to the front!" He
walked quickly to the office, a bounce in his step.

"Here's your check," she said. He reached for it, his "happiness on overload." Ripping open the envelope, he pulled out the

check, dreaming of his new bicycle and having groceries. The check was for $13. "At that very moment I felt like something had taken everything in me except my sudden dejection. As I went home I felt so empty."

Cecil's father eventually moved the brothers in with their Uncle Ed. "My uncle live in what they called a shack," he wrote. They all slept in the same room. There was no toilet but instead used an outhouse, where in the summer the flies swarmed around. But at night they wouldn't go out, but used a little pot called a slop-jar. The square footage of the shack was small, but the ceiling was very tall, and the roof was covered in tin, a comforting sound in a light rain. Once, however, a big storm came up with large hail. "As it hit that roof, it sounded as if it was going to destroy the house," he wrote. There were other problems in the winter because the whole house would be so cold until the old wood stove was filled and lit.

Uncle Ed's life was "basically about going out getting food, wood—truly only the necessities for living each day. He never said too much, he was always busy doing something outside." Cecil and David didn't go to school much while living there, instead going with Uncle Ed on "long trips down railroad tracks and through woods to get food. They also went to junk yards, collecting anything salvageable. "Uncle Ed did his best to take care of us, we knew he loved us," Cecil wrote, "but we were too much for him."

While they were living with Uncle Ed, Cecil met a girl at school who he liked. When he was at his grandmother's house, where there was a telephone, he would call the girl. "Whenever her parents realize it was me, they would hang up the phone, because they didn't want there daughter having anything to do with me. Somehow they knew of my situation." Cecil spent time walking by her house, hoping to see her. He remembered this girl long into his adulthood because not only was she beautiful, but she was kind to him at school. "But I have to give up on her because her parents were determined to keep me out of her life. They moved and I didn't see her anymore."

When he did go to school, classmates laughed at Cecil and his brother for wearing the same dirty clothes all the time. He got into fights over their taunting and stayed in trouble. Cecil and David had no lunch money either. Smelling the cafeteria food, they couldn't afford became another reason to stay away from school.

Eventually the boys were shuttled out to the country, outside Mount Pleasant to stay with his Aunt Redbone and her boys— the chickens, ducks, turkeys, and peacocks were new to Cecil, but he loved living there. "She was such a wonderful person," Cecil wrote. "She knew our situation and always tried her best to help us. She bought us new clothes when she brought some for her sons."

There were some adjustments as Cecil and David wedged into the same bed with the other three boys. He recalled how sleeping at the foot of the bed was the worst position because of how much all their feet stunk. "You couldn't take a bath ever day there, for they didn't have running water." Their clothes were washed in a huge metal pot with a fire under it. "I had never seen anything like it but our clothes were always clean," he wrote. He would watch as she rinsed them in the huge barrels that were all around the house, which caught the rain. "Oh, Aunt Redbone could cook, oh my! Her rice-pudding and homemade biscuits was so good." Those years with her and her boys were a bright spot, one of the few times Cecil and David lived a family life with a warm meal every day, clean clothes, and happiness.

CHAPTER FIVE

LIFE IN THE BIG CITY

———

WHEN HIS FATHER CAME BACK AFTER TWO YEARS, CECIL DIDN'T want to leave Aunt Redbone's house. But Mr. Johnson made his sons move to Nashville to live with him and their stepsisters in a one-bedroom apartment. "In the beginning things seem okay," Cecil recalled. "We had been away from our father for so long we had started calling him by his name, but one time he had a mini-fit and demand we stopped calling him by his name and call him Dad or Daddy." Cecil and David were starting in a new school in a new town, living in tight conditions. "I were used to taking care of myself," he wrote, so being under his father's thumb again was not easy.

Cecil had just started high school, about five years ahead of me, when he experienced the newly integrated schools of the 1970s. It was a jolt for both of us, not that many miles or years apart. The white kids would sit on one side of the classroom and the Black kids on the other, he recalled, which is my recollection, too. In the country, his school had been only Black kids.

Before court-ordered desegregation in Nashville began, I was a solidly average student in a brand-new building, stocked with the newest books, air-conditioning, the floors covered with indoor-outdoor carpet. The next year, bussed across town, I sat eating my lunch miles away on old dark green benches that folded out from dirty walls, in a sweltering heat. Over just that one summer, I somehow shot up to be one of the top students in my grade. Back then I never wondered why my grades were suddenly higher than the average, why someone might be wearing unwashed clothes, or why their speech sounded so different from what I was used to. And I certainly did not wonder how the students and teachers who had been at that school must've felt to be infiltrated by a collection of white kids brought in on buses.

For my white friends and me, court-ordered desegregation had an element of choice in it, because private, presumably all-white schools popped up that year in Nashville and many parents opted for them, but for most Black children, integration was not under discussion, nor did it involve a decision.

My parents did not entertain the thought of abandoning the public school system and were staunch supporters of integration, even as their young naive daughter climbed up on that yellow school bus bound for the inner city. I didn't know that on that first tension-filled day of busing—when most of my friends were being driven in their mothers' station wagons to the newly opened private schools—that my daddy, even in his conviction about integration, had his eye on the school bus from a few cars back, as it made the forty-five-minute journey to a part of town I hadn't known existed.

In Nashville at the new school, and without Aunt Redbone, Cecil and David were back to wearing old, dirty clothes to school. The other kids ridiculed them, and Cecil would fight them; he was expelled at least once.

Every so often, Cecil's father would take the boys back to Mount Pleasant to visit people. One time stuck out in Cecil's mind unlike any other, when they went back because the child of his father's best friend, Luke, had died. Riding in the car home after the funeral, Cecil looked over at his father in the driver's seat. A glistening trickle had spilled down his face, caught in the light of an oncoming car on the two-lane highway back to Nashville. "It was a moment I will never forget," Cecil wrote, "the very first time I had ever seen my father cry." Then, David started to cry at the sight. "I was so stun to see such a hard person like my father actually crying. And it was the last time."

Living with his family in Nashville eventually smoothed out to routine. His father had a girlfriend, who Cecil called Miss Marlow. She had four children, and he became good friends with them; Miss Marlowe was nice to them all. "She was always kind to me," he wrote. "But I was not going to trust any more stepmother. So I was simply respectful and polite."

Cecil made friends and was working as well as going to school. David, three years his junior, was also hanging out with friends more, and their time together became less and less. Cecil's work hours were long, but at sixteen the pieces of his life seemed to be coming together. He had gotten a second job, and soon his father told him he needed to start paying to live there with him. Cecil decided to move out because he "felt if I was going to have to pay rent, I might as well be out on my own."

The manager at his job, Stanley, was looking for a roommate at his apartment near Tennessee State University, so Cecil moved in with him. It took a while to save enough money to buy a mattress to sleep on, but little by little they furnished the apartment. "Everything was coming along well," he wrote. "I hadn't even thought about going back to my father—or school. I felt like I knew enough to take care of myself." Late one night when Cecil and Stanley returned to the apartment, they stepped into a scene they couldn't believe. They had been robbed, and everything of value that they had painstakingly bought over the months was gone. The place was ransacked. "For days, neither of us said much," Cecil wrote. But then Stanley dropped a bombshell and said he was going to start over somewhere else. Three days later he was gone, leaving Cecil with the entire rent bill due in two weeks.

The first time I had an apartment of my own I was a college graduate, and because I had an unspoken safety net, had I been short on rent, it would not have occurred to me that I would not have anywhere to live. But Cecil knew he was his only safety net. Always resourceful, and not wanting to admit defeat to his father, Cecil knew one way out. Some of the older people he had met in the apartment complex sold drugs, and they liked him. Cecil, looking younger than his teen years, was the front guy, who sat on the porch of an abandoned house to sell it while two men bought bricks of it and bagged it up.

The men were kind to Cecil and wanted him to go back to school. He didn't want to because he was making more money in one day than what he was making in two weeks at his regular job. Every time he suggested quitting that job, they wouldn't let him.

"They both cared about me," he wrote, not realizing that their concern for him had only to do with their profits. "They kept teaching me and I was learning."

During that time, Cecil started to smoke cigarettes, "one thing I wish I hadn't learn." Soon he had plenty of money and opened a bank account, depositing $2,000 in just a short time. To show his father he was making something of himself, he went to see him with his new clothes, shoes, jewelry, and wads of cash in his pocket. He gave his father $100 of it.

At Cecil's new job, the men would take as payment things like televisions, stereos, and jewelry. One night someone broke into the apartment to rob them; two people were shot, and the police came. Cecil, who had a small pistol on him, heard the police coming, so he crammed the gun under a couch cushion. "I had to think fast. I started acting like a little kid. When they asked if anyone else was in here, I slowly stand up. They ask me what I was doing behind the couch and in a little kid's voice I said I had went to the store for some guys here and when I brought there things in someone started shooting so I hid behind the couch."

"Did you see who was shooting?" the policeman asked Cecil.

"No, I was afraid to look," Cecil squeaked out.

"Well, what do the guys who live here look like?"

"One guy was light skinned and very tall," Cecil lied, cool as anything. Then the police told him to go home, never checking his pockets—where they would've found more than $1,000 in cash.

When his employer heard how Cecil had handled that, "he was so amazed and happy that he gave me all the money I had made for him that day. They kept asking me if I was okay and I was." Cecil had so much money at that time that he bought whatever he wanted, until the man told him to stop because it was drawing unneeded attention.

Late one night, Cecil was walking home to his apartment, along the edge of the road, when a car roared up, stopped, and a man rolled down the window. He was looking for drugs.

"What kind do you want?" Cecil had asked.

"A dime bag," the man said. Cecil had one, so he reached into his coat pocket to get it out, only to look up into the barrel of a shotgun.

"After they had my attention with the gun," Cecil wrote, "two other guys came out of the car." They took his leather coat, shoes, drugs, money, and a gun.

"One of them push me down and the driver started yelling SHOOT HIM!! SHOOT HIM!!" But right then another car's headlights appeared, and the assailants jumped into their car and took off. "I just knew that I was going to die," he wrote.

His employers asked Cecil what the men and the car looked like. "They sent me back home. After they found them, I never knew what happen," he wrote, but after that they all parted ways. When I was the same age, I had not ever had a gun pointed at my face, and still to this day, I have not been robbed at gunpoint.

Not even of legal age but on his own, Cecil got a job at Tennessee State University in a kitchen. He was then living in what he called a "boarder house," where he made some friends, one a woman named Dixie, whose boyfriend was Billy. "We treated each other like family," he wrote. In fact, when she moved home with her family, he did too, so much were they like siblings. He stayed there about six months, but when her brother needed to move back home, there wasn't room for Cecil there anymore.

In this group that felt like family, Cecil, an outsider, was made to leave once again.

With no place else to go, Cecil moved back in with his father, where he met the next-door neighbor's daughter, who was in town from Atlanta. In his memoir, he refers to her as Mrs. C. She told him she was starting a business. "She asked me if I wanted to be a part of it, and I thought she was joking." But soon he received a plane ticket in the mail from her. There was an address and telephone number to call when he got to Atlanta.

Cecil was surprised but with nothing much tying him to his life in Nashville, he raced around packing and left in a hurry for his first airplane ride.

He made his way down the long airport concourse, boarded, and settled into a seat by a window. When the plane started moving, he could not take his eyes off the runway and then the clouds in the sky and how the earth below looked like a patchwork. "I was overflowing with excitement and wonder," he recalled. When his ears popped and he suddenly couldn't hear, he panicked because he did not know to expect that. People stared at him, and, eventually, someone told him to hold his nose and blow, and then his hearing came back.

Mrs. C and Mr. C at that point were as good as their word, filling Cecil in on the new business and what his role would be. "The way they talked to me one would've thought I had a college degree and millions to spend." It was not a small operation; many people were already employed. Mr. and Mrs. C explained how he could buy into the company, and they bought him a new suit and gave him a room to stay in. His first event was a swimming pool party they gave for the "members" to discuss new fundraising projects. The idea they were pushing was to put horse and buggies on the streets of Atlanta, catering to tourists. Cecil passed out fliers and went with the couple to talk to people about financing. "After they seen they could truly trust me, they started teaching me more ways to make money," including learning how to make long distance phone calls without paying for them. "The first time they showed me about insurance fraud, I didn't know what was going on. I thought they were moving, but they were putting it in storage. Once they were ready, we would go out to eat for an alibi and a story." On their way out the door they would bash what was left, throw things around, and make it look like it had been broken into.

"Once they call the police they put on an act that could have won an award," and the insurance companies would always pay them for the "stolen" goods. "They were teaching me all sorts of things," he wrote.

Mr. and Mrs. C were not always in agreement, however, and many nights he heard them arguing. Fighting was normal for him to hear, but one night they sounded more serious, and Mrs. C was threatening to leave and to "spill the beans." Cecil, having had plenty of experience with family fights, and sensing that he was soon to be left on his own again, knew what to do. The next morning, he got up for work as usual, but after they had left, he took all the money that was in the vault. "I didn't even stop to get my clothes," he wrote. "I simply got on a trailway bus and went back to Nashville." Showing up on Dixie's doorstep, she took him in. Cecil soon realized he had developed real feelings for her but found that it was not reciprocated. "I didn't let her see it," he wrote, "but I was totally crushed." Then, once again, he went to his last but only choice—his father's.

Living with his father was different this time. "I wasn't the same person. I had learned how to make money and I use my newfound talent and put it to work." Based on his work scamming people in Atlanta, Cecil devised an elaborate scheme involving selling fake tickets and posters advertising a new club where $5,000 in prizes would be given away at the opening. "The money started coming in fast—faster than I had anticipated," he wrote. So much that his father thought he was selling drugs because of the kids who were bringing money to him. The bogus club opening had been set for nearly three months away, but he felt like he needed to end it sooner. He had $3,500 by that point, enough to skip town on a bus and go stay with his mother, which had been his goal.

He had hoped to make enough money to be able to go live with his mother, who by that time had moved out of state to Kentucky. Even after all she had said to him, he longed to be a part of her life. He approached the idea with a sense of inevitability that this must just be how a mother-son relationship *is*. "I haven't seen my mother in years," he wrote, "and it was so good to see her and she was glad to see me. I hadn't seen Judy, Angela and Darlene since they were little girls. It was a very nice reunion." He was surprised to see that his mother had chilled out and had "given the girls the freedom to speak freely without punishment. This took some getting used to."

Cecil was nineteen by this time, and with his mother's newfound openness, he was learning a lot—more than he wanted to know, but he listened intently. She told him he had had an older brother who was killed in a house fire, but she never told Cecil his name. She told him that before he was born, when she was about sixteen, she was raped. "Back in those days, no one said much of anything when something like that happened," he wrote later. Cecil listened in shock as she confided that he had another sister because his father had had an affair, and that his stepmother had recently had twins with his father. "I learned much more about my mother, but she didn't know too much about me." Not even that he was hiding nearly $3,500 in her house.

He had made a new friend (who we'll call Marcus), which was a big deal for him in a new place where he didn't know anyone but his family. At nineteen, Cecil looked more like sixteen, with no facial hair and weighing in at one hundred and ten scrawny pounds. The two of them started spending a lot of time together, "running the streets"—Marcus showing him the ropes and meeting more people, doing drugs, and drinking.

Cecil and Marcus were bored one day a few months later, drinking and trying to figure out what to do next. Marcus suggested joining the Army, so they went to the recruitment office and signed up. Cecil's mother was so happy. Before they did that Cecil went to the bus station downtown and walked over to the lockers to his usual one, #11, to check on some personal items he had stashed there: two black suits, two pairs of business shoes, and a briefcase full of his ideas for his next money-making scheme. The next day he went for the physical with Marcus right behind him. Cecil made it through, but Marcus didn't.

Sitting on the plane to Fort Dix in New Jersey, Cecil was not afraid. When his ears popped from the altitude this time, he knew exactly what was happening because of that flight to Atlanta. But once he got to the base, he soon realized he did not know what he was in for. When a very tall guy with a "Smoky the Bear" hat, the drill sergeant, came into the room with all the recruits to bark instructions, he started to regret enlisting. His head was shaved, and he got in line for the vaccines—one on each side of him, performed with a gun-like machine.

"Don't move!" the guy on the left barked. But Cecil flinched and ended up with blood running down his arm. That evening Cecil got into the first of many fights. He and his group made it through marching all day every day, punishing workouts, and all the things that Basic Training involves. Finally, they were granted a leave.

The Flamingo Club was dimly lit and filled with a loud bass beat that carried everyone into relaxation and fun. Cecil felt so out of place and was too nervous to talk to any women. He leaned against the wall off by himself and watched while everyone else was having a good time. He decided to have just one drink, which led to more. When it was time to go, his friends helped him into a cab, a scene hazy in his memory. The picture of that night sharpened for Cecil about the time they were back in the barracks, and the sergeant made a surprise appearance, calling them to formation.

"PUT 'EM OUT," he barked, about the cigarettes a few of them still were holding. Cecil, not fully understanding, kept holding his cigarette. "That was the beginning of trouble, for sure," he wrote. Someone touched him on the back to get him to put out the cigarette, but he thought he was being hit. "So, I hit the closest guy to me and that started the chaos, three or four confrontations erupted." Cecil didn't remember what all happened next but does recall waking up in the supply room with two other guys. Soon he was taken to confinement. "They said I hit an officer," and as a result, he stayed in confinement for nearly five months. While there he was still required to work out and have K-P duty every day.

After his hearing, he learned he would need to stay in confinement a whole lot longer—unless he chose the one other option, a medical discharge. As it had happened, when Cecil and his brother, David, were young, they had been playing with a sewing needle that somehow ended up in Cecil's leg, broken off and unremovable. That was his means for a medical discharge, which he chose. He went right back to locker #11 at the bus station in Nashville and picked up his tools for his con games again. He printed posters for a fake concert—this time saying that the band Earth, Wind & Fire would be playing— and presold tickets to people and businesses. The week before the scheduled concert he put the word out that it was cancelled, and the money would be refunded. But by that time, Cecil and the money were nowhere to be found.

Even Marcus had not known about the concert scam. "When I was selling drugs they had taught me to always keep my business on one side and my associates on the other," Cecil wrote. "From my youth I had already stop trusting other people."

Soon after, Cecil was riding around on a Sunday in a car with a friend, drinking wine, when they saw a young woman standing by herself at a bus stop. They pulled over to give her a ride. Cecil thought she was cute. He offered her a joint or a beer; she chose the joint and said her name was Marion Bogle.

She spent the night with him and as he was about to take her home the next morning, she burst into tears. She told Cecil that she had run away from a bad situation at home, and Cecil's father then allowed Marion to stay there with them. "That's when we found out she was only seventeen years old," Cecil wrote. But she stayed with them about a month until Cecil told her she needed to leave because he was also going to move out from his father's. She was ready for him with another bombshell, this time one that changed his life. She told him she was pregnant.

"I knew I had to do the right thing and marry her," so Cecil called Marion's mother to discuss it. Her mother agreed she could stay there. Cecil also learned that this was not the first time Marion had left home. Cecil was running out of money, so he set out to "get a real job. I couldn't keep doing what I had been doing because I had a child on the way."

Stunned and exhausted by Cecil's story, I took a break from reading, stuffing the pages back into the brown envelope and wondering how all that pain could fit into such a small space. It seemed impossible that the thoughtful man we knew had come from these hard, debilitating, and confusing circumstances.

CHAPTER SIX

GUILT (MINE)

———

AS WE CONTINUED VISITING CECIL, WE WOULD HEAR EVERY NOW and then that his mother and some of his sisters had come to visit. His mother later died while Cecil was in prison, and he had been relieved to have been able to see her there, although he knew he caused her pain by virtue of his circumstances.

"Over the years I have not forgotten the moments when I heard my mother crying in pain and grief on the telephone for me," he wrote. "Even through my own battle (my struggle requires much strength and focus) I instantly put my problems aside and did all I could to console my mother. I felt the need to ease her worry, to lessen her many tears and soothe away her pain. I knew I needed to do this, no matter how much sorrow I felt while hearing her crying as she attempted to keep talking to me, telling me how much she loves me and misses me."

That was a lot to bear. But what a testament to the power of love, that he had moved past all he had endured with her as a child. He also told us about others who had befriended him since he was locked up.

Rev. Joe McGee kept coming to see me even though I repeatedly told him I didn't trust him. He often asked me if I needed anything and I always said no; even if I did. I had so much more to learn about people, about life and I recognized it through the kindness I kept encountering from people I didn't know. I was beginning to comprehend that all people will not deceive you. ... Ms. Anna Mae Snyder came into my life speaking about the lord and being a friend to me. ... Still it took some time to feel in my heart that some people really will care about you without having some type of scheming motive.

Cecil's father visited him a few times. "The day came when my faith, my love in Christ would be tested, it was the day my father came to see me. It took so much for me to remain civil, to not [discuss all the things I knew he had done]. As he talked to me, I wondered how could he face me and keep a straight face. As he continued to talk, silently I asked myself *why have my father been the cause of so much hurt in my life.* Somehow I talked to him and he couldn't even sense from the tone of my voice that something wasn't right." Later he found out that his father had "fathered another child and named him Cecil Johnson. That would have been understandable if I was already dead. Momentarily I thought that my life was cursed, but I knew better."

It was about this time that Alan and, a little bit later, I stumbled into Cecil's life. He wrote, "I was blessed with new friends, the Robertson family, and it didn't take me long to realize that they are good people. They took me right into their family, treating me as a member. I had learned through Joe and Ms. Snyder that not all people wasn't untrustworthy."

So then our family had this little secret—we knew someone on death row, and not only that, we had what might be called *a relationship* with him. By that time, Alan and I had read the stories of his upbringing and understood more about him than most people. We had developed an empathy for him. But that didn't mean we discussed it a lot outside the family, although if it came up in conversation with people, then we would elaborate if necessary. You might not be surprised to learn that this doesn't naturally come up in conversation, even in the South. Visiting a death row inmate really has a downside because there just isn't much credit handed out for it. If you teach inner city children to read, feed hungry families, go on a mission trip, or ring a bell at Christmas to collect money for good causes, people will say, "Wow, you really are doing God's work, thank you!" And you are. But *way* down at the bottom of the pile of doing good deeds, and discussed only in whispers, is caring for prisoners accused of doing terrible, horrible, and unforgivable acts.

Unforgivable? That's one of the sticking points.

It turns out Jesus was in favor of forgiveness, and that's a tough concept to adhere to, especially if you are the person wronged. I get that. I hold grudges; I am a grudge-holder. I mean, I can stay mad at my husband for *days* over what later seems like the dumbest things. Yet when I consider forgiveness even if I am totally within my rights to continue to be angry—I *deserve* to feel how I feel—I come back to Jesus's radical notion of forgiveness, even when I don't want to. Ugh, why does he do that to us?

With Cecil telling me about talking with his father, listening about all the siblings he had who he didn't know, or his father's current life—I saw forgiveness in action. I was so angry with his father, and I didn't even know him. And yet, somehow, Cecil was able to move past the old hurts. My relationship with Cecil was teaching me a deeper understanding of forgiveness, which was frustrating. I mean, a lot of times I *want* others to pay, to hurt, to suffer, when they hurt me or my people.

My friend, author Joy Jordan-Lake, explains it this way in her book, *Why Jesus Makes Me Nervous: Ten Alarming Words of Faith*, which I found helpful:

[Jesus] turns, in his own final hour, to the thief on the cross, a guy who surely stole more than one loaf of bread—a career criminal. But when the thief rips his fellow criminal on the third cross for ridiculing an innocent man, Jesus, and begs to be remembered when Jesus comes into to his kingdom, Jesus says, translating loosely, "You are *soooo* coming with me. Today. Right now. Paradise."

It's anything but fair, or predictable, even.

Jesus makes it look easy, this kind of forgiveness of the thief on the cross. He's also asked the Father for forgiveness for the network of folks who put him up on that cross in the first place.

But suppose we put ourselves in the place of the crowd at the foot of the cross—not Jesus's cross, but the thief who's just turned to Jesus. He was trouble all right. He stole your car and totaled it on the way out of town. Stole your laptop and all your data, which cost you your job. He dated your sister, got her pregnant, and messed up on drugs. She's still paying the price. And although you can see from the pain on the guy's face that his repentance is real, that maybe he really is sorry and smashed up inside; still, you don't want anybody speaking comfort to him. To you, maybe. And to your family. But not to this guy.

It is simply not *fair,* Jesus's letting this guy tag along into eternal reward. The longer I live, the more I remain bewildered and befuddled by that. And also, desperately grateful.[1]

Coupled with this lack of credit for doing good deeds—and the need for secrecy because I didn't want to get reamed out in the grocery parking lot for being soft on crime—is that I didn't ask for this job. On some days, I absolutely can see why people might not be on board with this ministry because I wasn't either, at first. Most times, it's easier to hate than to understand and love. But I didn't figure that out right away or struggle with the concept. I do guard my thoughts on this subject because some friends, family, and acquaintances do likely think I'm a horrible person for "siding with a criminal." In practice, ambivalence and avoidance often proved to be the easier way to go. And, if you want to know the truth about it, I still carried some of that in me, too.

I kept Cecil at arm's length for a long time. Once we had Caller ID on our telephone, that was easier. I would always answer if we were uncertain about the timing of an upcoming visit or if I knew Cecil would have a question or instruction about what I was buying for him. But sometimes … sometimes … even into years of our friendship … I would let that phone ring.

We sat at the dinner table, finally, after a long day at work and an hour in the kitchen. Deep breath. Prayer. Pass the peas. The phone rang. All four of us froze, serving spoon in mid-air, my eyes darting from the salad up to Alan. No one breathed or clattered the silverware because the answering machine was two rooms away in the bedroom, so we strained to hear. My heart sunk, and struggling, I knew we were about to hear the mechanical prison man's voice announcing that he had a call from Riverbend Maximum Security Institution. It was him.

I felt torn. *The man is in prison; it's his only call of the day. What kind of heartless person am I—of course I will jump up and answer.* And yet, I have not talked to my family, with all of us together, for the whole day, or maybe, even in two days. We have finally landed here, all in one place, before we scatter again. Cecil has thirty minutes allotted per call, and that's how long we talk every time because he wouldn't want to waste the call on just a couple of minutes. If we took the call, the family would be gone from the table, my plate cold when I got back.

Although these were reasonable boundaries, later it's clearer that we should have always taken the call—who cares if dinner is cold, if the kids have scattered temporarily, that's nothing compared to where Cecil was—but in the moment, it was not as obvious.

On one of those calls that I did answer, Cecil was in serious pain because of a tooth. The dentist had been there, and it sounded like a similar issue I had had the month before—a root canal that resulted in a crown, medication, and follow-up care.

He didn't want to talk the entire thirty minutes because of the pain, and he was worried about the long night ahead with the throbbing. When that had happened to me, it was a simple fix with a prescription, so I was feeling a little impatient with him.

Me: "Just go ask for some ibuprofen or other pain meds!"
Him: "Where do you think I AM???"

Right, I thought, as I was jolted back to the actual situation. He told me that the dentist only came every so often, and it was already the day after the dentist's visit, so he would have to wait about six days before his tooth would be examined again.

Many weeks later the tooth was finally pulled, leaving him unable to chew well.

I recalled this disparity when a couple of years after that, Cecil and Alan both tore tendons in their arms. Alan had good insurance, surgery, pain medications, and extensive physical therapy, while Cecil was told that it would "probably heal on its own." That seemed barbaric to us, but Cecil or his prison mates didn't seem to question that or, like us, assume any right for decent health care. That was not the same for us. We insisted on pain relief, getting everything "fixed," without hesitation. He was not in that position then, nor had he ever been in his entire life.

At the prison visiting area, we met many of the men and their families who lived in Unit 2, greeting some of them warmly each time like old friends because we had shared these Friday nights and had seen the sadness on the faces of their family members. Alan would always hug them, especially Pervis Payne and Erskine Johnson, Cecil's buddies. They shared a friendship like brothers, and with Erskine, a love of art. Erskine would tell us about his latest painting, always with that big smile. As with Cecil, I was struck every time, wondering how anyone could smile like that living under those circumstances. At that time, I did not know why Erskine or Pervis were there.

Often at the end of visiting hours we would walk back to our cars with mothers, girlfriends, children, and ministers. Many of the families lived far away and had to travel hundreds of miles just to see their loved ones for a couple of hours. I felt sad every time we left, but these relatives had such searing pain, holes in their lives, I could not imagine what that was like for them to leave. When we first began our visits, I was able to observe everyone's feelings with sympathy at a distance, with detachment. But years in, I had begun to feel that deep sadness when we said goodbye.

Pervis maintained his innocence for more than thirty years. On November 23, 2021, after a vigorous, long-term defense by Federal Public Defender Kelley Henry, Pervis was formally removed from death row where he had been imprisoned for a crime he always said he didn't commit. He had been facing execution in Tennessee, despite living with an intellectual disability. The Shelby County district attorney conceded that Pervis was a person with intellectual disability and therefore could not be executed. She announced her office would stop pursuing the death penalty in his case.[2]

Sometime after we met him, Erskine changed his name to a Swahili one, Ndume Olatushani. I learned Ndume had been convicted of first-degree murder in 1985 at age twenty-seven, with no physical evidence, much like Cecil's case. In 1999, the Tennessee Court of Criminal Appeals found that the prosecution had violated the Brady Rule in Ndume's case and suppressed evidence.[3] The court, then, vacated his death sentence.

With that, Ndume added to a positive statistic. Since 1973, more than 185 people in the U.S. have been released from death row with evidence of their innocence. An average of 3.94 wrongly convicted death-row prisoners have been exonerated each year since 1973.[4]

Cecil was happy for Ndume when he was moved off death row, but, of course, that meant Cecil didn't get to see his friend anymore.

In 2004, Ndume was resentenced to life with possibility for parole. He was released in 2013,[5] about four years after Cecil was executed.

CHAPTER SEVEN

THE DEFINITION OF FAMILY

SITTING ON THE FLOOR OF OUR LIVING ROOM, MY MOTHER AND ANNE Grace were playing jacks when the phone rang. "GranAnne" was staying with our girl for the evening while Alan and I went to dinner. Anne Grace hopped up to answer, dialed a number, and began to talk, happily, as if she were talking to someone she knew well.

"She was carrying on this conversation," my mother recalled, "and I began to wonder who she was talking to."

Eventually, Cecil said to Anne Grace, a little worried that a five-year-old might be alone, "Is anyone there at home *with* you?" She said "yes" and handed the phone to her grandmother.

"I had figured out who it was before I got on the phone," my mother said. "I was surprised but was not worried about her talking to him. I thought that was kind of cool."

When my mother took the phone, she and Cecil were both laughing. "I introduced myself, and he said he was Cecil. We talked about why I was there with Anne Grace. It was friendly, and I felt like we had a connection." It wasn't long after that that he sent a gift of a cross made from matchsticks, one of his specialties, to her. "I don't think I talked to him ever again," my mom said. "But after that time, I felt like his friend, too."

"He would call a lot," Anne Grace said more than two decades later, "and we would joke all the time." Allie recalled everyone always passing the phone around to get their turn talking with him.

When Anne Grace was in sixth grade, there were several so-called friends who made her life difficult; it was an upsetting time with them bullying her in a "mean girl" way, leaving her out and making fun of her. We didn't talk about it to people in general, but her problems came up in conversations with Cecil about how school was going for her. He was troubled about how these girls were treating her.

"What do you mean they are leaving her out?" he demanded. "Ain't nobody better be mean to that girl! Do I need to come have a TALK with them?"

I smiled at his fatherly protectiveness and that for the moment he talked as if he had forgotten where he was. Amid my help-lessness, it did make me feel better that those girls (and their parents) would be scared to know that a man on death row was mad at them and had Anne Grace's back. It was all I could do not to mention it to them.

He would've made a good, present dad, but he or his daughter did not get to find out.

I think of my daughter growing up without me for the majority of her life. Now she is an adult and despises me for not being there for her. Nevertheless, I keep remembering hearing the sound of her soft voice as she spoke her very first words to me on a visit and the look in her little innocent eyes as she looked at me with a love I have never received before. Remembering how I felt when I touched her soft little hands and felt her grab my hand in return, how she cried when she did not want to leave me, grabbing my arms and holding on until she is compassionately forced to let go. Remembering the look of need and hurt in her eyes as she cried, looking back at me while being carried away from me.

When I read these words years later, I am transported back to the night when we took Allie as an infant to meet Cecil. I could tell it was important at the time, but I had no idea the depths of his complicated pain involving his daughter.

I missed her each day, days adding up to years—years without me being by her side when she needed me most. Regardless of what I must endure I am compelled by an undying love for my daughter. I continue loving her, because she is a part of me, praying every day, every night that one day she will open her heart to me and see that she has always been loved by me, always will be.

There was a time after his wife, Marion, died when Cecil didn't get to see Deangela for years. When he learned that his brother-in-law was taking care of her, he was upset; he wrote, "Without thinking and being grateful that my daughter had someone to care about her, instead I allow ignorance to guide my hand and took it to court," he wrote. He wanted his mother to have custody of her.

"I will never forget the day that I went to court about it," he recalled. "I hadn't seen Deangela in years, and she had grew so much. She wouldn't even look at me, nor in my direction. I was not prepared for what I heard next. I was in complete shock as I listen to my daughter tell the judge that she felt uncomfortable around me and that she didn't want me in her life. That hurt me more than ever before. I could not believe my ears and still she would not even look at me." His ride back to the prison was a quiet one, as he passed the buildings of the city he had not seen in so long. "By night-time my heart felt completely bewildered," he continued. "I didn't know which way to turn, I felt truly stripped of everything that meant something in my life. With all my might I tried to contain my emotions … but I felt my tears running down my face, one after another one. Never had I ever felt so empty, so alone."

During one of Alan's early visits, Deangela was also there; this was before the court custody actions and they were on good terms. A young teenager, he remembers she was shy, but that may have just been because he was someone who she did not know. He recalls how she and Cecil talked and laughed together. Cecil was so happy, proudly telling Alan about her accomplishments. He was so happy that she was there with him, even for a short time. He must have felt so helpless to keep her from harm, unable to be involved in daily decisions like parents who are present get to do—like when Anne Grace was seventeen, she decided she wanted to pierce her nose.

"Just a little, tasteful one, like [recent American Idol winner] Jordan Sparks," she had said to me. We had said "no" and argued against it. She then determined that the day she turned eighteen that she would just go get it herself, when she wouldn't need our permission. I pondered and then discussed it with Alan to come up with a plan. About eight months out from her birthday, I picked her up from school and drove the opposite direction from home.

"Where are we going?"

"To get your nose pierced."

"Funny, Mom. Don't tease me. Where are we going?" When we drove into the tattoo parlor parking lot, her eyes were wide, and she stopped accusing me of a mean joke. Alan and I had decided we would let her do it and take the credit for something she would do defiantly in a few months anyway. It would take the rebellion out of it. And I didn't want her to go alone.

The lobby was well-kept and clean, and reminded me of a dentist's office. Except for the walls, which had floor-to-ceiling drawings of tattoos, and the books on the coffee tables were not *House Beautiful* or *Ladies' Home Journal*, but pages and pages of more tattoo choices. She was drawn to the wall, studying a large butterfly. I watched her as I handed over my drivers' license for the receptionist to photocopy, a requirement that I found to be both alarming and reassuring at the same time.

"Don't push it," I said over my shoulder.

My daughter has a high tolerance for pain, so we were both surprised when piercing cartilage turned out to be much worse than a shot at the doctor's office. As the needle punctured her skin, pushing all the way through the side of her nose, tears rolled down her stoic face, and she looked faint. I knew then, that although I did not particularly want her to have that piercing, that we had made the right decision because I was there with her. And on the way home, she called all her friends to brag—and for a very short space of time we were the Best Parents Ever—except in Cecil's overprotective estimation. He did not appreciate that one bit.

"*You did what*?!" Cecil's voice was stern and loud on the phone later that week. I had expected a negative reaction from my mother but hadn't even tried to sugarcoat it for him. I just mentioned it in passing. "Why you do something like that? She has no business having a ring in her beautiful nose!"

"Well, it's not a ring; it's a tiny stud, almost, uh, tasteful, like Jordan Sp—"

"Am I going to have to come over there and straighten this out?" he said. "Put that girl on the phone!" You would've thought we had taken his baby granddaughter out and had her entire neck tattooed with a cobra. Unspoken, of course, was that he could no more come over and straighten it out than anything.

He probably had not had a similar conversation with his own daughter in decades, if ever. It may have been easier to parent a kid he wasn't related to. And he did not let it go, as I learned in his next letter to me:

5/3/08
    Hi Little Sister,
    I hope that everyone is doing well, that means you, too. Miss ya. Just in case you were wondering, I know I'm not going to see ya any time soon. ☹ I'll keep praying about it, maybe you'll give me a pity phone call. … Hopefully I'll see ya before the year ends. …
    By the way, when you see me again, I may have a nose-ring. Is that okay with you? Perhaps I'll do that next weekend, better speak up now! Ha ha OR forever hold your peace. Ha ha ha.
    How is your mother-in-law? I hope that she is much improved. I miss my mother, as I write these words, I can hear her voice in my mind.
    Well, I better close here, stay strong in your faith.
    Much love, Cecil

He loved being a father but did not get much chance to act as one, so if he took that job seriously with Allie and Anne Grace, we just counted it as a good thing. When his daughter was eighteen, he had been on death row for about sixteen years, missing all the highs and lows of parenting. He would've given anything to be a part of Deangela's life like that, and when our girls came along, he experienced a little of what he had missed as a parent.

"He would always say he would be coming over," Anne Grace said. "Or that if I didn't do something, like get an A at school, he would show up in the cafeteria. I would say, 'No, you're not,'" and because they called each other Shorty, she would add, "and if you do, you'll be too short!"

Despite all that had transpired with her custody and living arrangements after the court custody hearing, Deangela and Cecil were on good terms when she was older. She eventually had a son and a daughter and would bring them both to visit him. When he and I talked on the phone after his grandkids had visited, I could hear the absolute joy loud and clear through the phone. He reported in great, proud detail every movement or cute phrase the kids had said.

CHAPTER EIGHT

THE CRACKS IN OUR WALLS

CECIL HAD TOLD US THAT IF HE HAD NOT GONE TO PRISON, THEN he would be dead. Prison saved his life. How is that possible? He and I talked several times about how the life he was leading had been going in a dangerous direction. But after years of being locked up and finally getting some perspective and faith, he felt he had a relatively good life. This was something I could not imagine, but compared to the rest of his hard life, prison had just been a stepping stone in his life's rocky journey. One of those good things was meeting the person who turned out to be the love of his life. And he couldn't wait to tell us.

When I heard the robotic voice on the other end of the line, I was ready. It was August 2008, and I was waiting to hear from Cecil, so I could tell him some news: Allie had been thrown from her horse and had fractured a vertebra. She was eleven and would heal relatively quickly, but at the moment, I was home with her as she convalesced and watched a lot of videos. Sixth grade was about to start, and we were consumed with figuring out how she was going to do that. It was big news. I knew he was going to be extremely concerned and probably berate us for allowing her to ride. Instead, his jubilant and rushed voice filled the space.

"Now listen, I know what you're going to say, little sister …" he rushed in. Amid his laughter, he told me that he had gotten married. MARRIED! And not only that, it happened on 08/08/08, of which he was particularly proud. It was the same date as Allie's accident.

He was absolutely correct that I was going to give him a hard time. In addition to his marriage to Marion, Deangela's mother, who later died after he was in prison, he had married again while in prison, "hoping and thinking that I could start a new beginning." That woman's name was Shannon, and it was rather abrupt. When he first told me about Shannon, I was surprised they had married. He barely knew her, and they had not been corresponding very long. It was unclear to me at the time how they met or why he did that, but after two months, they separated (we have to disregard the terminology here, of course, because even when they were married, they were not physically together). When they soon divorced, he was heartbroken and angry, and later said, "It turned out to be one of the biggest mistakes in my life."

He knew I thought he had rushed into that and didn't even mind me saying, "I told you so." He said, "I know, I know!" Even though many years had passed since Shannon, when he told me about his new marriage to Sarah, I started right in, but he stopped me short.

"Don't even bring that one up," he said. "This one is different." And he was right, as I discovered for myself in the next year and a half as she saw him all the way until the end, pressing every possible angle to stop the execution. They had known each other for more than two decades, and she clearly was interested in what was best for Cecil, and he for her. She lived in Las Vegas, had worked with a ministry to death row inmates across the United States, and was a long-time CASA (Court Appointed Special Advocate) volunteer in Clark County, Nevada. Over the years they had developed a strong bond until they realized it had turned into love. That day on the phone, Cecil couldn't stop talking about Sarah and laughing because he was so happy. He told me how the Rev. Joe Ingle had performed the ceremony.

"I talked to both in advance to be sure it was a direction they wanted to head in," Joe told me later. "They were absolutely devoted to each other. Of course, they were aware of circumstances and the limitations on their arrangement."

Gathering in the visitor's area of death row on August 8, 2008, Sarah and Cecil vowed to love each other until death parted them; neither worried about when or how that might be. His early life of tragedy and hardship was redeemed just a little in this act of faith in each other.

"They really, really did care for each other a great deal," Joe said. "They were really in love. I didn't have any hesitation at all." Cecil made that clear in his next letter to me:

8/17/08

Hi Little Sister,

I pray that every one is doing well, especially little Allie. I have not forgotten how you and AG double team me [on the phone] either. I will get both of you back. ☺ Nevertheless, I enjoyed every moment.

Here is a picture of Sarah, your new sister-in-law. This time it will last, for truly we have much in common for sure.

I will close here, I thank the Lord for all of you ... you too sister. ☺ Much love, Cecil.

He was right that we did come to appreciate and love Sarah. She sent pictures to him and to us and stayed in touch. He was always in good spirits after getting to talk with her. She was his best advocate, giving him hope and keeping up with his case.

As we were finally paying closer attention, we reread some of his writings where he described his life as it was at the prison. As bad as conditions were, we wondered if that still seemed better than his life before.

I've watched the weather change more than most things, because the crack in my wall doesn't provide a chance to view much else. Most of all, I've seen myself change, growing from a childhood of abandonment where there was hurt, physical and mental beatings, hunger, tormenting loneliness, very little education, constant derogation, and seemingly relentless endeavors. I have experienced misdirected youth and ambitions, where I chased shadows and illogical dreams, had an inferiority complex and was self-raised and non-trusting. I have come from this into being a man who can see the vanity of life and the positive construction of a heart that reaches for the treasures of faith, wisdom and love.

Through this when you have read the things I've endured, you will have seen times in my life where I thought it was my willpower that helped me survive. I know differently now. Those were the times when the Lord carried me and was with me, just as he is with me now. This is what I hope you will see as I allow you to look in the crack in my wall of this world I dwell in.

A few months later in October he wrote to us about the last appeal in the process for him:

Here is the latest news on my case. I'm headed into my last court, if I don't get any help here, things may start to look a bit bleak, but don't lose your faith, you will have to stay strong with me. I will never give up hope, I have strong faith and I trust in the Lord. My spirits are the same, just in case you didn't hear me, my spirits are the same; joyful and strong. What is going on with you?

What was going on with us was much less serious, but centered on Anne Grace choosing a college, graduating from high school, and beginning to say goodbye.

It was the spring of 2009. Standing in the kitchen on the phone with Cecil, I listened quietly as he told me about the latest update in his case. Every movement seemed to take him closer to death, which I suppose had been the way it was ever since we first met him, but now I couldn't help but notice. We discussed it; I was vaguely aware of the process—that every appeal that gets denied is one more check off the state's list toward execution. He had one more court appeal, then a slight possibility that the governor could intervene. His concern—before he would tell me the latest denial or setback—is always in how *I* would take it. I'm sure he took this same tactic with family members and other friends, too.

"Now I don't want you to worry," he said, "but ..." He finished with the bad court-related news, that one hope had been dashed, he waited for reaction, reassuring me. Maybe that gave him strength to support me and everyone else emotionally, but it must have been unbelievably hard for him to do that. He wrapped up by saying, "enough about that, I need you to do something for me."

His plan was to make a necklace and bracelet for Anne Grace's graduation present, but he needed the size of her wrist and a finger. At that moment as he processed his probable death, he chose to focus on making someone else feel better, to do something for Anne Grace.

"I would always get a card on my birthday," Anne Grace recalled later. "And necklaces, a cross or bracelets on Christmas." This was true for all of our birthdays and all holidays. Sometimes, he remembered our occasions better than we did. We were so important to him, but also, he had more unfilled time—time to think about his bleak situation. Time was just different for him, more vast and empty. This is a classic example of how doing something for someone else can enrich the giver as much or more as the receiver.

When I mentioned that Anne Grace was already asleep, he instructed me to go measure her wrist while she was sleeping, so it could be a surprise. I saw a piece of ribbon, grabbed it, and lay the phone down on the counter, his precious allotted telephone minutes ticking as I crept up the stairs to her room. She has always slept in complete darkness, no nightlight, and her disheveled room was like a minefield, so it was slow-going. Always out like a bear in hibernation, I wasn't too worried that she would wake up and scream at the looming shadow above her, but still my mission felt peculiar. Feeling for her arm, I wrapped the ribbon and held the spot where it met, doing the same around a finger with the other end. I made my way back down to the phone.

"What took you so long?"

"Are you crazy?" I yelled. "I nearly broke my leg going in there in the dark! Settle down, I got it." About a week later, a padded envelope arrived addressed to her. In it were two pieces of perfectly fitting jewelry, made of white braided cord, and a graduation card.

If we ever needed an example of a person's unconditional happiness for another, even in the face of his own demise, this was it. Cecil was wholeheartedly celebrating Anne Grace's launch from high school to her life of limitless possibilities, while watching his own life likely coming to a violent close. Her life was beginning as his was ending.

"In the card," she recalled, "he stuck a picture of himself on a hot air balloon."

PART TWO

THE
NIGHTMARE

CHAPTER NINE

SURPRISE! WE SHOULD'VE BEEN PAYING ATTENTION

134 Days Until Execution

———

CECIL'S RECOLLECTION OF THE DAY HIS LIFE CHANGED FOREVER, the day after the robbery at Bob Bell's Market, could not have been clearer. This is his story, an account so detailed, certain, and full of emotion that when I read it, I believed he was telling the truth. He wrote:

> *The day begin this way. I got up that morning and made plans to get together with Fran, for it was a holiday weekend. … I called over to my father, but when I call, my father informed me that the police was looking for me, I asked him for what, he said about some robbery. I started thinking about an incident that happened to me when my father and I were sitting in the car out in front a place I once worked, "Ed's fish& pizza" and four police cars came down on us all at once and in an instance*

their guns was drawn on us and they said not to move. Later they told us that they had the wrong person, I looked like a suspect they were looking for. Now here they were looking for me again ... so I told my father that I would be there shortly, after I arrived we immediately called the police. One officer came and asked me would I go downtown to answer a few questions. I had nothing to hide so I didn't see a harm in it. When I got there I sit in an office for sometime, up until someone of more authority came in the room and asked why wasn't I handcuffed. I said for what!?

They didn't read me my rights, did not answer questions, instead they started asking me where I was last night, I told him. He kept asking me the same question. Finally I got upset and ask why are they asking me all these questions. That's when the officers said something about the Bob Bell store robbery. I told him that I didn't have anything to do with that and that I didn't no anything about it, after I said that he stormed out of the room. More and more officers came into the room looking at me. Everytime someone say something to me I told them it wasn't me, they have the wrong person, but each time they got angry and left me sitting there. I sit there for the longest time, I thought it was getting cleared up, when suddenly the officer in charged ordered me to be put in a cell. As I left the room I saw my father in the hall. The next thing I saw was many lights in my face and cameras people seemingly everywhere. As I passed all the cameras, loads of questions came my way. As I had repeatedly told the officers, I said I didn't do this. After they took me to the jail house, they left me in a small room alone, minutes later they took me to a back room and made me strip out of my clothes and handed me some other clothes to put on. I told them that I didn't need all this, because this would all be straighten out soon. Still he insist that I put them on. They then took me in the back room with a place to sleep and a commode made with a small basin on it, where you got drinking water or wash your face. I couldn't sit for I was waiting for them to straighten all this out. Hours passed and they tried to feed me something to eat, I wasn't hungry. As I stayed overnight I didn't get no sleep as I expected to be released. I became very upset and everytime a officer came by I questioned him and I got no answer, I became even more upset, up to the point where I started telling them that I was going to sue them. They brought me breakfast and I threw it at them. That entire day, I threw every meal back at them. … I couldn't shave, brushed my teeth, washed my face. The only thing I had was a roll of toilet paper. I finally fell asleep, but when I awaken, I was even more upset because I was still there. … I felt like I was in a very cruel nightmare and I couldn't wake myself up.

… They asked me if I wanted to take a shower. That is when I got a chance to see the other guys that were arrested. I got a shower, but I was still full of anger. Some of the guys told me that I had been on TV for the last few days and that I was their number one suspect. I got as much information as I could get.

Finally an attorney came to see me, the public defender. [Note: This was Walter Kurtz.] *He asked me a few questions, then informed me that I had a preliminary trial coming up. I had never had one, so I didn't clearly know what he was talking about. He wanted me shaved and be cleaned up.*

In the preliminary trial I saw many of my family members and friends in the small courtroom. I thought how that I could get all this straighten out and I could get out of here, especially after he [Victor Davis] *told them he was with me on July 5, 1980, he testified that I didn't do this. I thought now this will be over with soon and I was ready to go. After the District*

Attorney accused me, it didn't take long before I was bounded over for trial. I couldn't understand what was happening, it didn't make any sense to me. Victor had just told them that I didn't do this, that I was with him. I didn't get to say a word about it and I thought that my lawyer would do something about it, but he didn't.

... Back in my cell I was privately informed later that one of the guys didn't pick me out of the line up and that the second person didn't either at first and in the second look he was told that I was the main suspect and then I was picked. Still there were no way of proving it. I was given another test, one which was ask to be given by my lawyer, a lie detector test. I knew I passed it even before my lawyer knew. I didn't know it was impermissible in court.

I was on a lot of media distribution lists as part of my job, including for Tennessee's Administrative Office of the Courts (AOC). The AOC sends many types of notices, news releases, announcements, and court opinions. After Cecil's last letter with the warning about things starting to look bleak, I wasn't sure what to expect, so I had emailed the AOC's public information officer, Laura Click. On May 22, 2009, she emailed back that she had learned that the U.S. Supreme Court had denied Cecil's petition for rehearing on May 18. She added that the state attorney general's office had not yet filed a motion asking the Tennessee Supreme Court to set an execution date. She cautioned me that things could change at any time.

A few days later, Attorney General Robert E. Cooper Jr., Solicitor General Michael E. Moore, and Associate Deputy Attorney General Jennifer L. Smith made a motion to set Cecil's execution date, which I also learned in another email from the AOC.

On June 8, Cecil's lawyers James F. Sanders and James G. Thomas of the law firm of Neal & Harwell, and Gary Feinerman with the Chicago office of Sidley Austin, filed a lengthy response. In effect, they said Cecil should be granted a new trial or be resentenced to life. They gave several reasons, including that it had taken so long to carry out the sentence, which was "arbitrary and capricious."

They called into question the reliability of eyewitness testimony, and they asked the court to review the Brady issue.[1] The Brady Rule says that once a prosecutor knows of evidence or information that could be beneficial in a person's defense, they must say it exists and provide it to the defense. Cecil's lawyers felt this had not been done. This had been the avenue that eventually resulted in Cecil's friend Ndume's release.

Sanders and Thomas had represented Cecil pro bono (for free) for about twenty-seven years by that time and, by their estimate, had put in *more than five thousand pro bono hours on his case.* I have worked with a lot of lawyers, and most of them do a lot of pro bono work. But this is truly remarkable, a lot over a very long period of time.

"I feel very strongly that everybody is entitled to effective assistance of counsel," Jim Thomas told me later. "It's an obligation of the bar, ultimately, to take on the pro bono matters." These legal maneuvers were marching on, and yet Cecil was able to focus on faith, like he wrote in this letter:

> *Hello Suzanne,*
> *I pray that every one is doing well and I hope that you are having a great day thus far.* ☺ *...*
> *I haven't heard anything from the courts. My lawyer expect it will be sooner than later. Know that my faith grows stronger. I'll never stop trusting the Lord.*

I hope you all have a wonderful and joyful 4th. I will close here, keep the faith; I AM!!

Love ya,
Cecil

And then on July 21, I got another email from the Administrative Office of the Courts. The subject line was "Order Setting Execution Date for Cecil C. Johnson Jr." My hand hovered over the mouse before I clicked on it. I knew this order was coming someday, so I don't know why it knocked my breath out like it did. When it popped up on my screen, I couldn't read it right away; instead, I folded my arms on my office desk to cradle my head. How long I stayed like that I don't know, but when I lifted my head up, the email was still there.

It contained the court's full order,[2] the upshot of which was that the court declined "to re-sentence Mr. Johnson to life imprisonment or to 'reach back' and grant his application for permission to appeal denied over a decade ago. ... Therefore, the State's motion to Set Execution Date is GRANTED. It is hereby ORDERED, ADJUDGED and DECREED by this Court that the Warden of the Riverbend Maximum Security Institution, or his designee shall execute the sentence of death as provided by law on the 2nd day of December, 2009."

Cecil had an execution date. That's when it hit me: I had not fully understood the issues his lawyers were working on, and this was real. As if a fog had rolled off of me, I saw that we should've been paying more attention to the details all along.

CHAPTER TEN

"WHAT A FAMILY IS SUPPOSE TO FEEL LIKE"

125 Days Until Execution

NOT LONG AFTER THE COURT ORDER, I RECEIVED THIS LETTER:

Hi Little Sister,

I hope that all is well with you and I pray that every one is in great health.

I'm enclosing an addressed envelope to my lawyer, I was ask to ask everyone I know who would like to write something in my behalf, to do so as soon as possible.

I look so forward to seeing every one of you all together, that will be a blessed day indeed.

I will close here, keep the faith.

Love ya,

Cecil

His lawyers had begun talking with the governor's legal staff about clemency and gathering letters from many people. As Cecil had asked us to, we had written a letter to the governor on Cecil's behalf. (As it turned out, I wrote the letter; Alan was unsure of whether or not he should, given his government position in the State Architect's Office, working so closely with the first lady.)

I had emailed Cecil's lawyer Jim Thomas to ask what exactly they were asking of the governor. He told me they were asking for a commutation from the death sentence, asking the governor to change the sentence to something other than death. Jim told me I should explain how I knew Cecil and anything else I wanted to say. "Except," he wrote, "I would stay away from arguing merits of the case."

That was easy. I wrote back, "Thanks. I don't know the merits of the case, so that's not a problem."

I wrote to the governor on July 30, 2009:

"Dear Governor, Although you and I have met several times through my husband Alan's work, this letter is different than anything we have ever discussed. I am writing on behalf of a friend who Alan and I have been visiting on death row. ... I am asking you to spare his life."

I pointed out what I knew about Cecil's childhood, things a jury had never heard.

Further: "Cecil has told me that he certainly was not a nice person at that time in his life and, ironically, being in jail saved his life. The Cecil Johnson I know now is a level-headed, kind, loving, Christ-centered person who loves his daughter and grandchildren. He loves our two daughters and refers to us as family. We talk on the phone regularly and both of our daughters have grown up talking with him, writing to him, and receiving letters and handmade gifts from him.

"There have been so many times when, through his faith in God and Jesus Christ, Cecil has brought light to our lives and given us hope to keep going. I hope you will receive other letters from those who interact with him daily because he is an inspiration to those around him—prisoners as well as the prison personnel. Cecil has worked in the kitchen in his unit for years, sending much of what little he makes to his daughter who is raising two small children. He is concerned for her as any loving father would be."

Then I turned to the mechanics of the death machine in Tennessee. "As you know, the death penalty in Tennessee has undergone much scrutiny in the last few years, the outcome of which is tenuous at best. The damning report from the American Bar Association found specifically in Tennessee that our state was not in full compliance with most of the benchmarks established to guarantee a fair death penalty system. It is beyond my understanding that a state could execute a person while these questions are left unanswered. Tennessee's own bipartisan Committee to Study the Administration of the Death Penalty also discovered major flaws and unfairnesses in our system. Until these issues have been fully explored and examined, please do not allow another person to be executed. I do not believe the death penalty is a deterrent, but even a person who agrees with this punishment surely would want to consider these studies fully before ending a man's life."

I addressed the other elephant in the room, that several courts had ruled on the case. "Having been immersed in the legal field for most of my career, I have a great respect and awe for the judiciary and the Rule of Law. I know Cecil Johnson has been through the system and has had his case heard by many smart and compassionate people. I don't take lightly this request for you to change the outcome from what these courts have ruled. I do not believe, however, that Cecil has had all the advantages available to all, and that in light of the misgivings of those who have studied Tennessee's death penalty system in-depth, this execution and others must be put on hold until these problems are rectified. You are bound to be familiar with these studies. Surely you have a shadow of a doubt that the system has not worked fairly in this case—that to allow an execution until you know for certain cannot feel like the right thing to do."

I ended by pleading with him "to look into the issues surrounding Cecil Johnson's case and consider carefully if you believe he has had all the benefits that our legal system should afford everyone. His is a life worth sparing. He has much left to achieve and give."

At about that same time that Cecil's lawyers had requested letters for clemency (mid-2009) and unrelated, the editorial board of the legal magazine where I worked approved a submission by William Redick called "Will Tennessee Fix its Death Penalty?"[1] It was a look at Tennessee's 2007-2008 Legislative Death Penalty Study Committee and related issues. The purpose of the committee and the gist of the article was that *people with interests on both sides of the discussion agreed* that the system was broken and needed comprehensive reform. Mr. Redick wrote:

> In a report released in 2007, the American Bar Association (ABA) comprehensively evaluated numerous issues relevant to the administration of the death penalty in Tennessee. ...
>
> Applying protocols or standards for "a fair and accurate capital case system that complies with constitutional standards," this ABA Tennessee Study made 93 recommendations for reform, only seven of which Tennessee was in full compliance.[2]

Of the ninety-three basic standards this national group determined were required to make carrying out the death penalty fair, *Tennessee had only mastered seven of them.* I found that jarring.

My co-workers and I began considering art to illustrate the article and, after looking through hundreds of images, chose a close-up of a dripping syringe. By using such a graphic image, I can see in retrospect that I was keeping an arm's distance from the discussion even at that point, not associating *that* needle with *my* friend. Some kind of defense mechanism, I guess, was keeping me moving along in my job by not connecting my personal and professional lives.

As editor, I generally stayed in the background, and I didn't write a regular column. I definitely didn't put my personal opinion out there. I didn't mean to do it this time either, but as I stared at that order from the court with my friend's name on it, something unlocked in me. This execution was a real possibility.

I started writing and couldn't stop. I wrote about our family's relationship with Cecil and about how my job was overlapping into my personal life in an uncomfortable way. The *Journal's* Editorial Board approved this column and published it alongside Mr. Redick's article. When it came out, I sent a copy to Cecil. I was concerned about what he would think since we never had discussed some of what I included:

It's an odd feeling to know this man on death row so well—to know a different side than is reported in the news—and also to be acquainted with the people who have studied and decided his fate. I have shaken hands with most of our state Supreme Court justices, chatted about the weather with some, laughed with others. I have interviewed, written about and edited articles by several judges who sit on the 6th Circuit

Court of Appeals. I talk to the Governor and Attorney General casually at parties once or twice a year. I think most of them would know me on the street and call me by name.

This is where I have a problem, where I feel a bit schizophrenic on the subject.

Cecil would be surprised to know who I know. He might wonder why I don't *do something*. But these connections don't help in this situation. My knowing these powerful people makes no difference to the process. And that's how it should be—more points for the Rule of Law.

But reading reports from the ABA Tennessee Study (on the death penalty) and the findings of Tennessee's 2007-2008 Legislative Death Penalty Study Committee—detailed in Bill Redick's article—makes me uneasy. It makes me really want the system to be "fixed," as the article suggests it needs, before my friend is punished. On the other hand, I have no question in my heart that the men and women who have dealt with Cecil's case have done so as fairly and appropriately as they are trained to do. They are people of character and morals, surely basing their decisions on the facts as presented and applying them to the law as best they know. Knowing that Cecil has gone through the system encountering these people should make me feel better.

But still I feel sick.[3]

I felt sick because although that was all true about the people involved in the disposition of this case, something somewhere had gone horribly wrong. I soon understood that if an original trial had problems, biases, or possibly even inadequate counsel, there is almost nothing that can turn it around. Even in all those years of appeals.

I was nervous to hear from Cecil after he read the column. Had I said too much? What if he didn't want people to know so much about him, like how he felt about the prospect of a last meal? When a letter came, dated September 5, I ripped into it.

Hi Little Sister,
I pray that you all are in great health and I hope that you are having a good day.
Read your article, pretty good to say the least. ☺ I can say, I didn't see it coming. ☺ ... I thank you for speaking out the way you did. I see I have a brave little sister. ☺ I'm proud of you.
I will close here, stay strong; I am.
Love you,
Cecil

I do not believe I am brave at all. Seeing that from Cecil put a lump in my throat and does every time I read that letter, to this day.

After my *Tennessee Bar Journal* column had been published, I received another letter, an email that surprised me:

Thank you for your comments about Cecil Johnson. I was his trial counsel. In that role, it has not been appropriate for me to initiate recent contact with him. I remember most of his trial with painful clarity. ...

I got involved by fluke. Before a decade-long sabbatical from the Public Defender, I had represented Cecil on a serious assault charge. After I left for an unsuccessful experiment in private practice, I was surprised when his father visited me about the homicide charge. It had been assigned for arraignment in Div. III Criminal Court and then-trial-judge A.A. Birch would sometimes refuse to appoint the Public

Defender to continue their representation until proof that the family had no resources. Cecil's arraignment had been delayed for him to gather letters from private practitioners refusing retainer in the case. Thus, his father came to me, and I, in a typical exercise of emotion and cash flow over sound reason, took the case for $2,000 cash and a never-to-be-paid balance. For this fee, I took the case through trial, the Tennessee Supreme Court, and certiorari to the U.S. Supreme Court.

This was, I believe, the first Davidson County Death Penalty case since 1972's *Furman v. Georgia*. Expertise was scarce. ...

Like all of my death penalty trials, the experience with Cecil changed my life, taxing a personal relationship, fueling cynicism, and testing my sense of vocation. I survived this with a renewed belief that killing is wrong, whether on the streets or through a Courtroom.

Please tell Cecil he is much on my mind. My Sunday School class will learn of him and seek grace.

—*Mike Engle*

I could see that Cecil's lawyer was a person who had tried and cared, not a monster. After I received this email, I started to wonder how all the puzzle pieces fit together. If Cecil was guilty, then the system, as agreed upon by the citizens of the State of Tennessee, had worked. But the more I learned about the various procedures and seeming missteps, the more I wondered. Alan and I didn't want to act like we were worried, either to the girls or to Cecil—something surely would happen to stop this—but we realized how little we all had visited lately and certainly not regularly. That "life had gotten busy" is about as silly an excuse as there is, but that was the cold truth of it, and although we talked on the phone frequently, we had not all been to visit as much as we used to.

The summer before we moved Anne Grace into her dorm in Knoxville, three hours away, we planned a family visit to the prison. It was not a simple thing because Cecil was normally allowed only two visitors at a time, and the girls did not have up-to-date visitation forms. When I told Cecil that's what we'd like to do and asked him to send the forms, his joy and laughter rang in my ears.

"I know you don't mean it."

"Yes, we do."

"Okay, sure, I'll believe it when I see it."

I hadn't even realized that, although we had visited in various combinations at random times, we had not all four been there together for a while. He counted the minutes to events like this with plenty of time to keep track, while I wedged our visits into a frenzy of soccer games, horse shows, and work, so I hadn't even noticed the gap.

Once the paperwork was in and approved, we set the date and drove to the prison. It was hot August for this "Special Visit," which is what they call it when you veer from the norm; the rules are bent a little for unusual circumstances.

The girls, who were then twelve and eighteen, had not been to the prison in a long time, but I could see flutters of memory every now and then as we signed the book, passed through the metal detector, and were frisked. Of all the procedures we went through to get in, they best remembered the purple handstamp and the curious light that made it shine.

"When we went the final time, it looked different from when I was younger," Anne Grace recalled. That day, fifteen years later, was different in many ways—one, in that it wasn't visiting hours for that lower security area at that time. So, when we walked through the larger room, it was deathly quiet and empty, the expanse of hard institutional floors gleaming.

The girls went through these motions with us: showing the handstamp, buying the snacks, and walking past the recreation yards toward death row. When we finally made it through the second door inside Unit 2, Cecil was standing inside the visiting room, waiting. I thought his face might split in two, his smile was so wide. He rushed us all in hearty hugs and stood back to admire the girls. His pride in them was so evident I could tell he felt ownership in their raising.

And that is true. He set an example, like remembering every one of our birthdays—every time—with personal homemade cards, and his ability to laugh and keep a heart full of joy in the face of a hard existence. He shaped their thinking in ways none of us realized, increased their compassion, and caused them to notice injustice in a way no book or lecture ever could have. I didn't have this realization until years later, however. On this particular visit, I was full of conflicting emotions about it all.

"I can't remember leaving the cafeteria building and walking to the other building," Anne Grace said later. "When we went that last time, I didn't know how to get there, didn't remember walking into the building in the smaller room." But the bookshelves full of picture books and toys, similar to the ones at church, were familiar to them even after all that time.

There were several other prisoners visiting at that time, so we sat in a corner where we'd never landed before, where rows of chairs faced each other a few feet apart. We pulled a tall, fat, gray trash can to the middle, popped its lid down tight, and placed the bounty of the vending machines on it, as if we had a coffee table. This became our den. Cecil didn't have time to bother with eating the popcorn or pie; he could not stop looking from one of us to the next and back around and laughing and saying, "*I cannot believe this!*" He probably never had a family game night—not with his parents and siblings or with his wife and daughter—and for this brief time in his world of clanging doors and execution dates, he was free and light-hearted.

The buttery smell eventually got the best of me; I opened the bag of popcorn, and we started eating. He peppered the girls with questions about school, their summers, and when Anne Grace would leave for college. One of us suggested playing UNO, so Alan grabbed the deck of cards from the nearby bookshelf.

UNO is a competitive game that requires you to disregard the feelings of the person sitting next to you, even if you might normally be a more compassionate player. Soon, Cecil was slapping down "Draw 4" cards with relish, and each time someone made a wicked play, he would laugh with his whole body. It really is a game you can't be nice in, and if you want to win, you must be actively merciless. So, when the girls started griping at each other about certain moves, Cecil would laugh all the more.

A few days later, we received a letter from him, and I then realized that the girls' squabbling only showed him how much we all love each other unconditionally. Bickering over a card game was music to his ears.

I must thank you for this last visit, for I felt so much love. I felt like a brother, a uncle, a friend all in one. I enjoyed every single moment and I will never ever forget the feeling I felt to be all together like that, I felt what a family is suppose to feel like. For nearly all my life, I have yearned for what you all gave me. My heart is still touched by all the wonderful emotions I experienced. I can never thank you enough. This is so strange, because I hadn't feel so much like that. I thank the Lord for our last visit, truly it gave my heart something new. I like the way everyone relaxed and had fun. I smile with mere thoughts of the memories. THANK YOU!!

Cecil thought about that visit a lot, I'm sure. He had written about his own experiences, and after spending so many years in reflection, seemed to have a clear picture of how things went wrong in his family. But as always, he found the silver lining:

So often I have wondered what my life would have been like if I could have grown up in a true home. I never truly got to really know any of my sisters, for we grew up in different homes and with different values. We all knew each other, but there was never a true bond. Still today it is so evident, because we all are so separated in many ways. When I see the bond between other siblings, I can't help but envy such closeness, such seemingly wonderful trust. Perhaps being alone during most of my adolescence and teens years is part of the reasons why I'm able to deal with my loneliness this place creates day after day.

As the days toward his execution ticked away, Alan and I were not only wrenching over Cecil's impending loss of life, but the related fallout: the pain his wife, daughter, and grandchildren, his brother, and our daughters had, too. We wondered how the victims' families must have been feeling. I sure hoped someone else was tending to them. They must have believed the person responsible for their pain was about to die, and one assumes they were glad for that, even after all these years. As for us, it was way too late to ask for a do-over—if we had known at the beginning what we knew at this point, would we have continued with the friendship? We had put the girls smack in the middle of this bizarre, painful thing.

"I remember knowing it was going to be soon," Anne Grace said of the execution date. "But I didn't think it would actually happen."

I catch myself at that thought that we did this to ourselves by getting involved, that we chose this path, putting ourselves into this ugly environment of prisons and sentences and killing. But how many people are in this situation who did not choose it, who are many degrees closer to the pain, say, of a father, mother, or son in prison? Our ability to step into or out of this world was just one more privilege we had.

That family visit turned out to be the last time Anne Grace and Allie saw Cecil, which Alan and I suspected at the time but had not said out loud.

"I realized I wish I'd gone more. I would've talked to him more," Anne Grace said recently, her sobbing taking her over for a moment. I asked her if she wished she had not been dragged into it at all, not been connected to this eye-opening sadness. I had wondered this for years but feared the answer too much.

"No," she says, struggling through tears. But her view of the world has been colored by it—surprisingly not by violent crime or the insides of a prison, but by the sentence of death and its related problems. Knowing what she knows has "made it harder," she said, and has given her a maturity she didn't really want. This is the kind of pain that can happen when we love someone up close, when we get into their lives and they bring us into theirs, when we show up for one another. The suffering and heartbreak are part of the risk when we reach out to make friends into loved ones, and when we are part of a community.

It sure is rotten how that works.

CHAPTER ELEVEN

CONNECTING WITH ANOTHER EXECUTION

7 Days Until Execution

———

IN ADDITION TO WRITING POEMS, LONG BEFORE WE MET HIM, CECIL had begun exchanging letters with some relatives and many new friends. These letters and his thoughts seemed to come together for him in meaningful ways, showing great insights that he hadn't known he could have. These were not always obvious, but he had gotten adept at understanding the importance of signs and symbols. So, when signals lined up, he paid attention.

He had, through interactions with many caring people, become a Christian and changed his entire way of thinking. He even stopped smoking and earned his high school diploma! He wrote about how that came about and how it affected him:

As days passed I kept getting all sorts of letters too, each of them would ask me to read some parts of the Bible, I read some of them, but not all of them. Then one day I received a letter from my grandmother and she also sent me some Scriptures to read. That is when I asked myself why so many people are asking me to read the Scriptures here and there. ... That is when I decided to read the entire Bible from beginning to end. There were so much that I had never realized and the more I read, the more I wanted to read. Often I had to ask how to pronounce some of the names, but I wasn't going to allow that to discourage me.

Cecil continued to study the Bible, searching for something.

I felt like so much was missing from my life ... and I knew without a doubt that I wanted to be save, that I wanted to be baptizes in the spirit of the Lord. I stopped indulging in drugs and committed myself to changing my life for what is right. I felt something inside of me pulling me away from my old life. ... It was like my eyes were slowly opening up for the very first time. I wanted to change and it didn't matter if I was in this place or not. ... On many occasions I would find myself worrying about things I truly needed. Nearly each time before I could come up with a solution on my own, my needs was answered by someone's goodness towards me. It happened several times before I realized that the Lord knew my needs before I did and were taking care of me as I realized He had been doing. In retrospect I can see farther back at the times the Lord had taken care of me and watched over my life, because on all of those occasions I would have surely lost my life otherwise.

As Cecil read that Bible late into the nights, a sliver of understanding took hold. He connected the stories from thousands of years earlier to those very nights that he was living through.

I stayed as busy as possible, still the silence of the nights opened doors to my soul. I couldn't understand all the things that had happened in my life and yet the Lord gave me strength to keep walking forward. ... As I begun to study the book of Job, I found myself forming a new perspective about life. Even though Job lost nearly everything, he kept his faith. That is when I realized that my faith was nearly nonexistent. Everyday for hours I studied the Bible and little did I know it was an old testament and a new testament. I didn't know anything about Jesus until I started reading St. Matthew.

I've been reading the book of Matthew my whole life—picture books even!—but had never had this light-bulb moment. And I never once related to Job, a character in the Bible who suffered much even though he was blameless. That story shows that innocent suffering does exist.

Learning about Jesus open my eyes, my heart. I will never forget the time I read where he was crucified, I lain in bed with tears running out of my eyes asking life WHY!! ... WHY!! ...WHY!! At that time I didn't understand that Jesus had to die for us.

Cecil did not grow up knowing the Bible stories, going to Sunday School, Vacation Bible School, or church camp like I did. These stories were drummed into me from the start to the point that I have often taken them for granted. *Jesus died for our sins*—yes, that was the phrase.

But the cold hard truth is that Jesus was *executed*.

When Cecil read this story, he made a connection far different than I had ever had. It was this kinship that likely strengthened him enough to get through the next rounds of appeals, even as the process began to move toward what looked like the end.

I never heard any details of the attempt for clemency, just that it was denied, and I never knew why. I have seen the governor several times since then, but we have never discussed the letter or its circumstances. I don't know if he read it or if he even knew who I was. Maybe he didn't have time to study the case closely, and there were bound to be political pressures, a Democratic governor in a red state. But I didn't understand how a person could know all the details and still allow the execution to go forward. With the denial of clemency, the process kept moving toward the execution, and soon I received another related email, from Laura Click at the Administrative Office of the Courts:

Sent: Nov. 25, 2009
Members of the media:
Cecil Johnson is scheduled for execution on December 2. As I receive notification of filings in either state or federal court, I will share the information with you. We will also be posting this information to our Web site. Beginning Monday, I will also be posting filing updates on Twitter. You can follow along at www.twitter.com/TNCourts.

The Monday morning after Thanksgiving with Cecil's execution still full steam ahead was that day I made my way out to the prison, alone for the first time. In my car on the way back downtown after the visit, I kept reliving our conversation, especially the part where Cecil said I was the only one he could not handle seeing cry. I couldn't figure out why that was.

Once in my office, I stayed close to my computer, refreshing my email every few minutes, hoping both to have a message about Cecil and not to have one. Finally, with no word all afternoon, I emailed Laura at the AOC. There had been a hearing set in the U.S. District Court of Middle Tennessee that morning. She didn't know the outcome yet but after a few hours sent word to the members of the media that Judge Robert Echols had determined that that court lacked jurisdiction and ordered the filings sent to the U.S. Court of Appeals for the Sixth Circuit.[1] At this point, there were roughly thirty-eight hours before the scheduled execution.

Not very far away from the prison, Cecil's wife, Sarah, sat with the Rev. Joe Ingle in a modest house, worn by time but battling its age with the help of a nonprofit called Family Reconciliation Center. The group provides a free place for families of prisoners to stay when they come from out of town to visit. It's called the Guest House.

Joe and Sarah were trying to figure out the next move for carrying out Cecil's wishes: He wanted to file a legal action that would prevent the state medical examiner from performing an autopsy on his body if he was executed. Autopsies were the routine for those executed in Tennessee, but Cecil felt it would be a desecration to his body. In addition to that, I thought privately, what a waste of time and money for the state. It seemed pretty obvious to me that when you shoot someone's veins through with poison to kill them, and they were otherwise healthy right before that moment, one could make the leap and surmise as to what killed the person.

That day Joe had talked to one of Cecil's attorneys, Jim Thomas, because Sarah thought he was handling the autopsy matter.

"It was very important to Cecil," Joe said, but they learned that day that the lawyers were not working on that issue. "That set off a mad scramble on my part for who could get this litigation together and file it," Joe said. "It was a crazy day." He asked Brad MacLean at Office of the Post-Conviction Defender, which represents death row inmates in post-conviction cases. He and his colleagues took the case to oppose an autopsy, filing in state and federal court.

"We had to move quickly and request the court to expedite the proceedings," MacLean recalled. With the clock ticking on that afternoon before the execution, the papers were drawn up; Joe and Brad took them to the prison for Cecil to sign.[2]

At the time, I did not know that the autopsy challenge was happening, but as the hours to the execution time got shorter, I recalled a poem Cecil had written years earlier. It seemed to be fitting at that moment:

"As I Walk"

Please my loving Father help me. This road I'm on show so little hope and compassion. Many times the nights seem like days and the days seem like nights. As you know I've come a very long way and it appears that I have a long and harder way to go. Help me to endure what I must and show me which way to continue.

Father, with faith my life is in your hands. My troubles and sorrows I pray to be abated. And ask to be shown the right way to go now; as I walk. I've come to the point in my life where the road I see, seems like mere days and nights of time merely passing away.

My loving Father, my heart is strengthened with the knowledge of Your love and goodness. Though there were many times when I didn't know, please help me to stay strong. The road before me doesn't show which way is right, nor how to walk. In my heart I know I must not stop. Guide and help me continue.

Father, throughout my life; You've loved us all. Please don't allow me to be lost by false feelings of forsakenness. I know there have been times where I've done things that displeased You. Look inside my heart, see that I want to do what's right. Please see Father that as I journey the road of life, I need You every day as I walk.

Cecil may have written that poem after he knew Joe Ingle, who had served as Cecil's spiritual advisor for years. But as the execution neared and Joe saw that it would probably actually happen, he realized he could not be there with Cecil through until the end. He had been in this death row ministry business a really long time, and it was taking a toll. He was exhausted with the futility of it all, and he was depressed. Years earlier, Joe had witnessed the execution of Willie Darden in Florida, whom he had been close to, and afterward knew he would not be able to do that again. After asking Cecil's permission, Joe called up his friend, fellow pastor Rev. James "Tex" Thomas, and asked him to step in.

"I was not there," Joe said of the execution. "I was not willing to do that. When you work with people and love 'em, you can't just stand there and watch 'em get killed."

CHAPTER TWELVE

TICK TOCK

15 Hours Until Execution

THE NEXT MORNING, ALAN AND I WENT TO THE PRISON FOR WHAT we knew could be our last visit with Cecil. His brother, David, was already there visiting, but the guards said we could go in anyway. We said we would wait, but David told them it'd be fine with him for us to come in.

We went through the same motions that I had done the day before, and there were the familiar vending machines; Alan was as amazed as I had been that the death chamber door was right there so close to the sandwiches and chips. We signed the guest book, and as that last door opened to the closet-sized visiting room, two middle-aged men turned their heads toward us and broke into smiles. David, who Alan had met once before, was standing as I had been the day before, the two plastic garden chairs pushed back into the corners. Cecil, on the other side of the glass, was so happy to have a gathering of guests, he looked like he was hosting a get-together on his patio. *Come on in!*

The brothers' childhood had bonded them closer than any circumstance could break apart, and each knew his brother's love would never end. They were reminiscing when we came in and stopped long enough for us to hug David and wave hello to Cecil.

"Do you remember that Christmas with the slippers?" David, continuing his story, said, and they both burst out laughing. Their mother had wanted some house shoes, and they were determined to give them to her. They had ended up stealing a pair because they had no money for gifts.

Another time, they recalled, one of their sisters had thrown a butcher knife at David, and they covered for her, so she wouldn't get in trouble from their father. The boys took the blame, and the beating from their father had been so severe, blood splattered on a wall. Tale after tale began to flow as they laughed—even as my mouth dropped open at the horror of some of it—and finished each other's sentences because they knew the stories by heart.

The brothers relived their childhoods and were proud to have each other's shared history. They hardly took breaths in between the end of one story and the start of the next, as they disregarded the unspoken shadow that this might be their last chance to be together. Witnessing the two of them, I would not have guessed about the abusive family, the hunger, the betrayals, and the other dysfunctions had I not already read Cecil's memoir. Every story they told had a boisterous punchline between them; an outside observer could see that the common thread was about overcoming terribly tragic circumstances, but that was not the focus that day. For a short time, there in that cold, hard room, there was warmth. To have a person in this world who understood every nuance of where he came from and what he had lived through was a gift no one else could give Cecil. His little brother who knew him so well was there when it counted, and we were honored to witness such a love. It is the most sincere and genuine family reunion I've ever been to.

The warden then came in, smiling, and we turned as he approached the open door to our closet-space.

"How ya doin', Cecil? Do you need anything?" he said, and we shook his hand to meet him like we were at a business event, a grand opening of the death chamber or something. As the warden turned to leave, I noticed the string that comes on a new suit coat—the one that holds the flaps together at the back until you clip it when you buy it—was still connected. It appeared that the warden had bought a new suit for the occasion, possibly even a career-defining event where he would be in front of a lot of media.

I shared an ironic smile and an eyeroll with Cecil after the warden left. I wanted to say, "Oh no, we're all good here! Couldn't be better—except for the part where you are about to kill my friend here—if you could work on that, we'd really be all set." The new suit reminded me of the media circus and the purpose of our visit. It was not a picnic or a proper family reunion. It was the last time we would see him.

A woman came and took Cecil's temperature, reaching through the mail slot.

"They want to make sure I'm well," Cecil said. "That's funny." We all laughed with him, a little more forced this time, realizing that the State cared only about his health because it would mean fewer complications when it came time to kill him. That rolled off Cecil easily; he had learned early in his life that the appearance of thoughtfulness did not always indicate real caring or sympathy.

On that last visit, while Cecil was waiting to hear from his lawyers in hopes of a stay of execution, he also must have been privately preparing to die, thinking about tying up loose ends. At least, that was on *my* mind.

Through the glass, I said, "After you're gone ... how—"

"No, we're not going to talk like that," he broke in, waving his arm.

"But what is your favorite hymn? Who will—"

"We don't need any of that. We can talk about all kinds of stuff next week." That's when I realized he was sticking full force with the line of thinking that the execution that night was not going to happen.

He had a lot on his mind, I know, but he acted like it was a jinx or bad luck to even discuss the possibility that the execution would happen. I did not want to talk about it either, but I knew we would want to know his wishes. He started talking about fishing, Deangela, and how his grandkids were doing—anything to fill the otherwise dead air. Finally, he slowed down, looked straight at me, and said steadily, "Tell Anne Grace and Allie not to worry about me."

As we prepared to leave, words didn't come easily for any of us. Visitation was nearly over; we wanted to leave first, so the brothers could have their own moment. The knowledge that it was fewer than twelve hours until the execution time hung in the air smothering us, with just a touch of hope floating nearby. Cecil put his palms up on the glass as Alan and I each matched a hand up to his. We sensed this was the real goodbye, and after a moment, we began backing away from the glass. Like the day before, I looked him in the eye and said "See you tomorrow!" as if it were just another day. But Alan is always much more direct than I ever am and knew he must say what was in his heart.

"I haven't ministered to you enough," Alan stammered, recalling the original purpose of their visits a decade and a half ago. "You always end up ministering to *me*."

Cecil just smiled and said, "See you, brother. And you take care, little sister. I love you both." We hugged David goodbye and left, signed out of the book, passed those damn snack machines, and went through the clanging gates to the cold outside.

Cecil had written a poem some years earlier, and he was probably feeling this way again on that day:

"Lonely Lonely Man"
As you can see I'm feeling
Truly empty and dismayed, many
Times I have tried to
Smile, though only a part
Of me is displayed. I
Know that You have heard
My heart, my prayers every
Day, every night. With the
Mere touch of your divine
Hand I'm positive that my
Life would change from pain
And loneliness to good, beautiful
And alright. As you know
I don't want or need
Endless wealth, nor the best
Of things in the world.
I only want and need the love
You have shown
My heart, which to me
Is worth more than gold
Or silver, diamonds or pearls.

My Lord what must I
Do to have one dream
Come true, to have a
Chance to share the love

That is really true. With
Every passing day a part
Of me is saddened away,
With every passing day a
Part of me is hurting
Away. I have prayed
Today and tonight, I will
Pray again. Please my Lord,
Make the loneliness, and
Pain all end. All I
Need is a touch of
Your divine Hand. If it
Is Your will touch this
Hurting heart, this lonely-lonely man.

That afternoon my mom and dad had picked Allie up at school, and they were at our house with her. Allie, a pre-teen, had not wanted to talk much about Cecil's impending execution, but we told her what we expected to happen and how we were hoping that it would not happen.

I went to my office after leaving the prison, planning to go straight from there to the first of two services that night: one was at a church and one was a candlelight vigil in a field beside the prison. Before I left, I checked my email again and found one from the Administrative Office of the Courts.

Sent: Tuesday, December 1, 2009 4:22pm
Subject: Cecil Johnson - Order from 6th Circuit
Members of the media:
The U.S. 6th Circuit Court of Appeals has denied Cecil Johnson's motion for a stay of execution. Attached is the

corresponding order. It will be posted on our Web site momentarily.

We will continue to keep you apprised of any additional developments.

I clicked over to see what the *Tennessean* was saying: "Defense attorneys filed an emergency appeal for stay of execution, along with a supporting memorandum," it reported. Among other things the appeal had said that the execution "would constitute cruel and unusual punishment in violation of the Eighth and Fourteenth Amendments to the United States Constitution and Article I, § 16, of the Tennessee Constitution," the story continued. "The motion for a stay calls for a consideration of procedural matters, over whether Johnson's subsequent appeal is a second appeal on habeas corpus grounds. Prosecutors fought against the stay, and the United States Court of Appeals for the Sixth Circuit has chosen not to issue a stay of execution."[1]

My first thought was "But the Tennessee Titans won with that mystery play!" Irrational, I know, but I pictured Cecil thinking the same thing when his lawyer gave him the bad news from the Sixth Circuit. There was still the U.S. Supreme Court, but I was not following the ins and outs of the legal maneuvers. There was always still the extremely slight possibility that the governor would change his mind.

There was still hope, however small.

Driving around in a part of Nashville I knew nothing about, I got a little lost looking for the church. It was dark and rainy. At several intersections, I fought the urge to turn around and speed home. But then I saw it; I was relieved and full of regret at the same time. I found a parking spot on the street, got out, pulled my coat around me against the damp cold, and headed for the front door of the historic building of Hobson United Methodist Church. The old building's concrete columns closed around me as I plodded up the steep stone steps toward the heavy wood door.

More people were milling around than I had expected, and as I waited for my eyes to adjust to the inside light, someone handed me a lavender sheet of paper with the order of service on it. "A Service of Remembrance and Resistance," it said. My plan was to slip in and observe from a back pew, but I looked up to see the Rev. Stacy Rector, executive director of Tennesseans for Alternatives to the Death Penalty. She smiled and came over to hug me. We had met on several occasions before, and I knew her story was similar to ours in that for years she had visited a man, Steve Henley, on death row. He was the person who had been executed ten months earlier, in February 2009. She was there for him and his family through that ordeal.

She told me there would be a time on the program called "Reflections" for people to talk about Cecil. "You are one of the few people here who actually knows him," she told me. "Would you consider talking about him?"

Uh, no way, I screamed in my head. That went directly against my back-row plan, and I sure didn't have anything prepared. I smiled weakly at her, saying "I don't know." She squeezed my arm, told me that either way was fine and that she understood. And I knew she did.

She moved on, and I begin to consider my seating options, scanning the sanctuary. Old, creaky, and beautiful, the dark wood pews were laid out in a semicircle, red hymnals sticking up from their racks on the seat backs. The carpet was also red, and I noticed the wide, two-story rectangles of stained-glass windows lining the side walls. They'd be bright and sunny in the daytime, but now they were dark and gloomy.

Glancing over the crowd, I saw a diverse group of people. The church was home to a mostly Black congregation, but tonight, I suspected that in addition to members of the church, there were many visitors, like me. The group assembling was eclectic— young, old, Black, white—and all of us gathered to protest state killing.

When my scan of the crowd reached the left side, about mid-way down, I felt a huge relief seeing our dear friend Jason Rogers. I made my way over to him, amazed that he was there.

"Elizabeth will be at the candlelight vigil," he said of my dearest friend, his wife. "She's home with the kids now and when I get home, she'll head out." I looked across the aisle and saw another friend, Melinda Medlin. She had visited an inmate on death row for a while, and we had shared stories. I went to hug her and felt firsthand how it does make a difference for people to care about what you care about.

This is what the "Ministry of Just Showing Up" looks like. I don't think that is a real term, but my dad talks about it (and practices it). It's as simple as it sounds: show up for people when they need you. Many times, I don't go when there is hurt because I worry that I will be in the way, or that I will make the pain worse with my sympathetic smile. I learned it by watching my parents, and I needed to remember Jason, Elizabeth, and Melinda on this night whenever I questioned if I should show up for someone or not. Just Showing Up counts for a lot, even if there is nothing to say, and it won't change the outcome.

I guess that is what we did for Cecil, too, even on that night. The flip side of showing up is that often the giver also gets a benefit. When I think of all the cards and letters and genuine caring that we received from Cecil, I know that is true. He showed up for us too, which confirms that even in the most restrictive of circumstances, it can be done. I took my seat next to Jason as the crowd was welcomed, and a time of silent reflection began.

Here's a little background on my relationship with God: When God talks to me, he often has to shout, push, and kick me to get me to notice. I don't mean to be so difficult for him, but I am not a person who lightly says, "God told me" to do whatever. I am too cynical for that and am wary of using that line as an excuse for what really may just be for what *I* want. Often, it's hard for me to tell if it's God or me.

This same old struggle was what was happening inside me, again, as the congregation went through a responsive reading and the hymn "Precious Lord, Take My Hand." The song is about being tired, weak, and worn out, and asks God to "lead me on to the light." As the decades-old plea rang through the chapel, it felt like it was directed at me. I fumbled in my purse for a pen. Voices rose up, singing about the end of someone's life, as they called out to God for help.

As the Call to Confession, Matthew 9:10–13, was read, I started to scribble notes on the back of that lavender sheet. That passage is about when Jesus was having dinner at Matthew's house and had brought along some folks with questionable reputations. Some righteous people did not like that and called Jesus out about it. He said, "Who needs a doctor: the healthy or the sick?" He went on to make the point that he was interested in inviting outsiders in, not just helping or agreeing with those who were already on the "inside."

I, then, heard someone reading Lamentations 3:22–24 in the background:

The steadfast love of the Lord never ceases,
his mercies never come to an end;

They are new every morning; great is your faithfulness.
"The Lord is my portion," says my soul, "therefore I will hope in him."

My pen was flying. I was jotting fragments of thoughts, jumbled up yet all suddenly so important. Music was playing, and people, one at a time, filed down to the front to read passages from Deuteronomy, Isaiah, Matthew, and this passage from Psalm 139:

O Lord, you have searched me and known me.
You know when I sit down and when I rise up;
you discern my thoughts from far away.
You search out my path and my lying down,
and are acquainted with all my ways.
Even before a word is on my tongue, O Lord, you know it completely.
You hem me in, behind and before, and lay your hand upon me.

Dang, every word spoken or sung seemed to be shot directly at me.

My eyes closed; I visualized Cecil's smiling face. He would've loved the service, with all the scripture, music, and, of course, because it was about him. I wanted to be able to describe each dear part to him, so he'd know how much he was loved. By this time in his life, he had finally understood that he was loved by many, but even still he would've been surprised and pleased at the turnout at that church that night.

The swirl of music started again, and Stacy invited people to come forward to share recollections. There was a long silence, and no one moved. Creeping into the back of my mind I heard Cecil saying, as he had told me years earlier, "Through the Scriptures I received strength and peace." Okay, okay, *I hear you.*

Then, I noticed my hand gripping the seat in front of me, heard the creak of the old pew and the floor as I rose and walked toward Stacy, and turned to face the crowd. As if I were watching myself in a movie shot from above, it felt more like floating, as I could not believe I was about to do this. I introduced myself and my connection to Cecil, and, steadying myself on the communion table I was standing behind, said something like this:

My husband and I were laughing our heads off with Cecil earlier today, if you can believe that. He and his brother were reliving happy memories from long ago, and we were privileged to be with them. He reminded us that he believed that God has specifically sent our family to know him because he said he "didn't get much of a family. God gave me a new one, so I could see what it was supposed to look like."

Cecil does not believe he will be executed tonight. But he wanted us to know that he will be fine either way. He has the promise of heaven, and he has hope. "You are looking at faith," he said to us, and we knew that was true. Faith, not so much in the legal system but in God, that either way, he will be fine. When we left the prison this morning, Alan said he didn't feel like he'd ministered to Cecil at all. As usual, Cecil had ended up ministering to us.

I sat down in my pew and put my face in my hands to think more about that. Cecil's caring had slipped up on us while we were pretending to be the ones supporting him. He had "shown up" for us all these years, inadvertently teaching us about unwavering faith, focus, and impenetrable joy. The guy smiled and stayed strong through a lot of crappy things. I prayed that we might actually learn to be more like that from his example.

In return, I believe we gave Cecil the unconditional love, permanence, and loyalty that he had never had as a member of a family.

After the service, several people came up to talk to me, including a newspaper reporter who wanted to interview me (I declined)—and a man named Mike Engle. I tilted my head back to look up into the face to meet Cecil's trial lawyer, towering above me in his tall, lanky frame. He was the man who emailed me after my column about Cecil was published, but at the time, I didn't connect exactly who he was, why he might have attended—or why he would want to meet me.

Melinda and I left the church and ate some dinner before the candlelight vigil, and we made the thirty-minute drive to the other side of town toward the prison. I have no memory of this dinner, my mind so focused and fuzzy all at the same time. Elizabeth waited for Jason to get home, and then she met us after we ate.

Five miles down the road from here, there was another dinner being served, what has been described to me as a "feast" for employees, witnesses, and others who were gathered at the prison for the execution. It was going to be a long, taxing night for them, too, so they had planned accordingly although that struck me as barbaric, to have even the appearance of a celebration. The food was not for Cecil, who had refused the traditional "last meal." He had told me he didn't understand that practice, so when the time came, he wasn't going to have one. He said he considered it "foolish if they are just going to kill you next."

"Good point," I had said to him.

CHAPTER THIRTEEN

FRIENDS IN HIGH PLACES

7 Hours Until Execution

A LITTLE BIT BEFORE THE HOBSON SERVICE STARTED, ALAN WAS wrapping up a meeting on the twenty-seventh floor of the Tennessee Tower in downtown Nashville. As assistant state architect, he had a lot of meetings up there in the first lady's conference room as they worked on the renovation of the Executive Residence and the design and implementation of Conservation Hall. He enjoyed his work on those projects very much, even when managing the contentious neighborhood opposition and political antagonism. He had a great admiration for the first lady, which only grew through the years as she exhibited grace under pressure in all these situations. She always asked Alan about his family, and she especially kept up with us in the years when his mother's Alzheimer's disease began to wear all of us down.

The meeting was running late, but Alan had already decided to skip the Hobson service. The whole process was taking its toll, and we agreed to meet at the prison vigil later. All the years they had worked together, he had never mentioned his relationship with Cecil to her, but on that night with the execution just hours away and close to his heart, he did.

"It was on my mind already because it was getting dark," he said. She was sitting at the head of the big conference table; he was sitting to her right, facing a bank of large windows toward the east. Down below was the War Memorial Building; to the left the Capitol; and creating a triangle with them was the John Sevier Building, another state office building, which at that time housed the attorney general's office. Alan knew that over in that building, lawyers would be working late into the night to fend off any last-minute hitches intended to stop the execution.

"There's something I want to tell you, and I'm not looking for you or the governor to do anything, necessarily," Alan began, "but I've been friends with Cecil Johnson, who I'm sure you are aware is going to be executed tonight. I have visited him the past fifteen years. Suzanne and our daughters have visited him, and it's been a difficult time."

They began to talk.

"She said 'I know it must've been hard for you,'" he told me later. "She asked how old Anne Grace was when she started visiting and thanked me for sharing all that with her."

Alan continued, "I told her I didn't get involved in his case. That I was simply there to be a friend." She told him she had complete trust in the court system and the attorney general, and she talked about how they did not take these things lightly.

When Alan told me this, years after the execution, I had just spent the day reading the appeals court opinions, news accounts about the crime, and learning for the first time some of the details about Victor Davis, the witness who abruptly changed his story days before trial to incriminate Cecil, instead of providing an alibi, in exchange for his immunity.[1] (Davis's original account, first given to an investigator for the Public Defenders' Office on July 8, 1980, was significantly corroborated by a totally neutral, third-party witness. Defense counsel disclosed Davis as an alibi witness months before trial, and prosecution investigators interviewed him at length, in which Davis did not waiver from his story that he had been with Cecil and they were not near Bob Bell's Market. But then things changed right before trial.) Thus, Cecil was convicted based only on eyewitnesses, one of whom swore the assailant had no facial hair, but Cecil's mug shot showed him with a mustache and goatee the next day.[2]

This remains problematic to me. I *want* to feel as the former first lady did, to continue to have complete trust in the attorney general, the courts, and the system. I do. And I *used to*. It's not even that I had had conscious trust in the system, but more that in my life experience, as a white person in the middle class, I had always assumed it was fair, that the cards were stacked evenly for everyone. In fact, it never occurred to me that it might be otherwise, such was my privileged, oblivious situation. But once I began studying it, it became obvious to me that the likelihood of a Black man with an ill-prepared lawyer and missteps early in the process probably would not have had the same outcome as I, had I found myself in similar circumstances.

"I felt good that I expressed myself and my feelings and emotions," Alan said of his talk with the first lady. "I've always felt close enough to her to go outside of business and talk about something like that. But I wasn't expecting her to be able to do anything." He knew where she and her husband stood. Alan probably felt the same reticence with her that I did in knowing the Supreme Court justices. The relationships were professional and not such that we would influence their positions just because we knew them through work.

From the twenty-seventh floor, where Alan and the first lady were, if you pressed your nose to the glass and cut your eyes to the left, you would be able to see the Tennessee Supreme Court Building. This is where members of the AOC staff had gathered for their long night, the court's Public Information Officer Laura Click told me. They stayed until they received a phone call saying the execution had been carried out. The Supreme Court clerk and members of the court were "on call" in case they needed to make any decisions. There was also a member from the court's website team to get everything loaded to the website, Laura told me, as well as a staff attorney to assist in explaining things. The justices on the court at that time were Gary R. Wade, Cornelia A. Clark, Sharon G. Lee, Janice M. Holder, and William C. Koch Jr. I have chatted, emailed, and done in-depth interviews with each of them over the years, but I have never discussed this subject.

I was thinking about the justices because in 2006, our magazine staff had been shooting the *Journal* cover photo of retiring justices Adolpho A. Birch and E. Riley Anderson at the state Supreme Court building in Nashville.[3] It happened to be on the same day as two scheduled executions—Paul Reid and Sedley Alley. (Alley's execution was carried out; Reid received a stay from the U.S. Supreme Court but later died in prison.) I described that day in an article:

As we waited for the photographer to set up his lights, Justice Anderson explained to me how he needed to be in Nashville that day anyway, as part of the "death penalty protocol," where all the justices gather in the capital city in case they need to have a late-night meeting. He mentioned matter-of-factly that moments earlier a stay had been issued for one of the men. Hmm, I said.

It struck me as unusual that I would be having this sterile conversation on this subject with him on that day. The reporter in me wanted to grill him on how he felt about it, if he was at peace with the system, if he could help me understand. Then, I wanted to pull Justice Birch aside and ask him how he was feeling, if he takes it to heart. Instead, the bar association employee in me went over to check with the photographer on the lighting. At that time, I didn't even know that Birch was the trial judge in Cecil's original trial, or I might not have been able to contain my curiosity.

Anderson said in that interview that the capital cases are the most difficult part of the job. "They're the hardest cases. I remember when it has been close. And I particularly remember when, as chief, I've been on a secure phone with the warden communicating about whether to go ahead or not. Those are pretty tough times," he says. "You tell yourself that you have a job to do, and you do the best you can."

Like Anderson, Birch said he found capital cases to be the most difficult.

"You know it's part of your duty, but it's not a pleasant part. It weighs heavily on you, but you simply tell yourself that your duty requires that you be involved and to the extent your duty requires it, you involve yourself. That's all you can do."

During the photo shoot, I made funny comments in an effort to get a chuckle or smile out of them. After all, the story was about their retirements and what they would be able to do next. They needed to look happy. But the weight of the day's execution business hung in the air, and they couldn't see much humor.[4]

These justices are at the heart of the legal system, upholding the Rule of Law. Even with all the system-wide problems and inconsistencies, I still want to believe it works. I've spent my career working in this world of law, acting like it's worthy of our trust, and I know it can be.

But it gives me pause to think that there was no DNA evidence in the murders at Bob Bell's Market, no weapon or stolen money ever found, and no surveillance video. Alan and I have talked so much about this, about our hopeful belief in the reliability of the justice system, honest human error, and how tempting it might be to gloss over the incongruities to get to the end result.

"Before you execute somebody, you've got to realize our system is not perfect," Alan said, again wishing there had been some DNA evidence involved in Cecil's case, now that it would be possible to confirm things. I reminded him about my research and the disconcerting things that I had read about all the pieces that just didn't add up.

Alan was walking to the kitchen to take a dirty dish, but stopped, turned around, and said, "You mean they could really execute someone if there was no video, no DNA, no weapon found, and the witnesses were unreliable or changed their stories?"

"Well, yea," I said. That's what was happening to our friend.

Back at the Guest House, Sarah Johnson was waiting with the Rev. Joe Ingle. She had had her last visit with Cecil in the afternoon.

"We were waiting to hear from the court to learn if [a stay] would be granted or not," Joe said. "I was dealing with funeral home people, letting them know we didn't want an autopsy.

There was a lot up in the air as time ebbed away there. It was your basic painful, awful situation [waiting to know if] the man she's cherished and loved would be exterminated."

Joe said there was "a real dissonance" earlier in the day in how Cecil was dealing with the impending execution, and I remember that as well. He would not talk about a funeral or any details that would suggest he would die that night. I imagine he just could not think like that, as he pushed all his energy and faith into believing it would not happen.

As time ticked away, Joe got "two or three calls" from Brad MacLean with the changing circumstances in state and federal court in the [autopsy] litigation. "There was a huge amount of uncertainty, a huge emotional drain," Joe told me later.

"Cecil doesn't think he's going to be executed," Joe said, and that made it hard to prepare. "Sarah doesn't want to believe he's going to be executed. I was trying to support and prepare her. She was distraught. All you can do is be there with somebody. We prayed. We talked if she felt like it," he says. "It was a very hard evening."

Back in 1990, nineteen years earlier, there had been a glimmer of hope, one of very few in this entire process. A juror from Cecil's trial came forward and said in an affidavit that she had not understood that she could have voted for life in prison. She thought she only could choose the death penalty. One of the appellate decisions reported it:

She thought she would have to explain her vote to the judge if she voted for life; that she was afraid the judge would look at her and say, 'Well, why did you do it?' [and] that she was not afraid of the judge but was afraid that she would be embarrassed.

The juror further stated that she now believes, deep down in her heart, that Cecil Johnson did not commit the crimes.[5]

The affidavit had no effect. In his May 3, 1982, opinion, Justice Cooper had noted that it "is settled law in this state that a juror cannot impeach her verdict, and that a new trial will not be granted upon the affidavit of a juror that she misunderstood the instructions given the jury by the trial judge, provided the instructions were correct." The Tennessee Supreme Court therefore had affirmed the sentence of death and post-conviction relief was denied.[6]

I wondered where that embarrassed juror was on the night of Cecil's execution and if she now realized that being uncomfortable talking to the judge wasn't a very good reason to keep quiet on an issue with this much at stake. But it was too late, the court said. *You did what you did, and it's in the record now and cannot be changed.*

CHAPTER FOURTEEN

PROTESTORS

5 Hours Until Execution

A PAIR OF BLACK, INSULATED BOOTS SPEND MOST OF THE YEAR on a shelf in our utility room. Sometimes when I pass by them, I think of Cecil and that night he died. I bought the boots December 1, 2009, the day before his execution, knowing the vigil outside the prison would be cold. *What does one wear to an execution vigil*, I had wondered and smiled, knowing in all its inappropriateness, Cecil would've laughed that I was being ridiculous to worry about shoes. In the store I hadn't been picky about the style of the boots; the main purpose was warmth. I still wear them in winter, and those around me have no idea they are execution boots.

Melinda and I met Elizabeth to ride out to the prison after the service at Hobson Methodist before the execution, leaving her car in a restaurant parking lot. Elizabeth arrived with a coffee thermos, cups, and snacks, which warmed my heart as much as my hands. Driving the long, industrial road out to Riverbend was disconcerting on a normal day but was worse that particular night under the circumstances. The road came to a dead end right past the prison, which I had not known before. I had always turned left into the flowing driveway up the hill toward the prison, never curious about what lay farther on. At the end of the road, we were directed by security personnel to park in a field to the right, shown to our row with flashlights as if we were at a county fair. We loaded ourselves down with folding chairs, blankets, and Elizabeth's treats, and walked across the road. Alan would meet us there later, he'd said.

A sign read: "Protestors, keep right." As if I didn't already have a feeling of dread, the addition of protestors was just going to make it worse. Why would someone come out and taunt us at this terrible time?

But *everyone* was going to the right, including all the people I recognized. Wait. *WE were the protestors?*

Of course: we were protesting this execution.

A tent stood in the field at the bottom of a slope that led up to the prison buildings, about a football field away. I could see the parking lot up there where we'd been earlier that day with the circus tent for media and the tall lights surrounding the building; each had little halos around them in the foggy night. Volunteers with Tennesseans for Alternatives to the Death Penalty were handing out flyers with instructions about "honoring life by abolishing the death penalty." It included specific directives:

We will use our anger at injustice as a nonviolent force for change. We will refuse to return assaults, verbal or physical, of those who oppose or disagree with us. We will refrain from insults and swearing. We will protect opponents from insults or attacks. ... We will not damage property. We will not bring or use drugs or alcohol. We will not use threatening motions. We will carry no weapons. If arrested, we will behave in an exemplary manner. Our attitude as conveyed through words, symbols and actions will be one of openness, friendliness, and respect toward all people we encounter, including police and corrections officers and others.

A loud hum from portable heaters kept the deathly quiet away, and people stood and sat, murmuring and offering encouragement to one another. Posters hung on the nearby fence said things like, "Execution is not the solution," "The death penalty is a failed public policy," and "God does not approve of the death penalty. –Martin Luther King Jr." Someone offered me a chair, but I didn't want to sit down, as if pacing and being more uncomfortable myself would help more. With Cecil up that hill preparing to die, I just didn't think I should be relaxing.

I couldn't take my eyes off the prison, picturing each building's doors, the gates, the fences, the vending machines, and the death chamber. Just that morning I hadn't planned to be at this vigil and assumed we would be at the execution itself. But then we had learned that we would not be allowed in, much like the visit the day before when I only got in through a special request of the friendly guard. We were not technically family, media, or an otherwise approved guest, and therefore, we were not on the list.

I never knew if Cecil knew that ahead of time, or if, when they wheeled him in on the gurney and he scanned the seating area behind the glass and saw his daughter, wife, brother, and lawyers, that he thought we had chickened out, or worse, didn't care enough. He would have also seen some reporters, his new spiritual advisor, the Rev. Thomas, and the father of the twelve-year-old boy who had been killed.

Cecil and I had not discussed the possibility of whether we would be there because he didn't think it would happen and didn't want to spend time on the subject. That night I felt guilty to be in that field and not closed in the viewing room with his real family, reporters, and representatives of the victims. I was guilty for not being there for him even as I felt guilty for being thankful that I was not present too. (Six years later, I discovered the form on the Department of Corrections website outlining who is eligible to attend an execution. This list includes lots of official people like the warden, the attorney general, the media, prison chaplain, defense attorney—plus immediate family members of the victim and the condemned. There's no category for "friend," which Cecil would've realized. He would have known we could not have been there without a special request from him. Reading that, I felt a slight pressure lift.)

Surrounded by a group of about a hundred anti-death penalty crusaders singing hymns and praying, I was thinking about how we were not in the chamber where Cecil could see us. I was vaguely aware of a photographer, who turned out to be from the city's newspaper, as we gathered in a circle for prayer as the time of the execution approached. I stood, my back to the prison, with the group for a while until the drumming in my head became too loud.

Theirs was a global protest, which I appreciated very much, but ours was personal. Usually when a loved one dies, everyone— friends, family, doctors, nurses—works feverishly to keep them alive. This seemed to be the opposite. We were about to lose a friend who people were actively *not* trying to keep alive, and the sadness was intense.

The governor had already denied Cecil's request for clemency,[1] so there was just one shot left. On the afternoon of December 1, just hours before the scheduled execution, the U.S. Supreme

Court discussed Cecil's case, to decide whether to issue a stay. Justice Clarence Thomas and Justice John Paul Stevens had a heated discussion about the length of time Cecil had spent mired in the court system, and not unsurprisingly the two justices disagreed. I don't know why they weren't talking about the shaky witness situation or lack of evidence, but they were not. CNN reported that although the stay eventually was denied, Stevens would have granted the stay, along with Justice Stephen Breyer. Stevens's issue was that too much time had passed after sentencing and before the planned execution. He said he felt it amounted to cruel and unusual punishment.

"Johnson bears little, if any, responsibility for this delay," said Stevens, who said procedural hurdles at the appellate stage for capital defendants created what he called "underlying evils of intolerable delay. The delay itself subjects death row inmates to decades of especially severe, dehumanizing conditions of confinement."[2]

Although Stevens had supported the resumption of the death penalty in the 1970s, his view had changed since then, and he had expressed his opposition to it. The CNN report continued with Justice Thomas's take on who was responsible for the long process. He said that Cecil Johnson had created the delays himself by challenging his conviction for twenty-nine years. By using these "procedural safeguards," Thomas asserted, the delays are just part of it.[3]

The fact not mentioned was that twelve years were lost because the prosecution did not turn over all the evidence until forced.[4] Whether that would have changed the outcome is debatable, but it did add extra years to the process, not by Cecil's choice. That evening Justice Thomas suggested that there are alternatives to the process that would speed it up, if Justice Stevens did not like the delays. He reminded the court of the centuries-old English custom of carrying out an execution the day after conviction.[5]

I didn't know about the justices' discussions at the time, or later at 12:38 a.m. Central Time when they issued their statement. I was standing in a field with a candle in my hand. I turned and walked toward the prison. I couldn't get very close because of the razor wire, and that wasn't my plan anyway, but I was drawn toward it, feeling like a heavy rock was pressing on my chest.

It began to rain. As the clock ticked and no one's phone rang to say there had been a stay, I pictured myself curling up on the muddy ground in exhaustion and sadness. Apparently, I was still standing, though, because I soon felt an arm around me. It was Alan, who had followed me out there. We cried as the time of execution had long passed. I watched the sky above the prison glow from all the extra late-night lighting, thinking I might see Cecil's soul drift up. When I did not see it, I imagined it. I could see him bounding up some cloudy steps into the stars.

About a hundred and eighty miles to the east, Anne Grace, a freshman in college, was alone and also watching the clock. Allie was, I hoped, asleep at my parents' house. Anne Grace had not felt comfortable talking with her roommate or other friends, for fear they would deride her or at the least, not understand how she could even care that a man convicted of such terrible deeds was, at long last, about to get his due from the government.

From the comfort of all these years later, I wonder why we didn't make more provision for Anne Grace and her feelings that night. Allie was in town, unlike her sister, but too young to go to the prison. She was with my parents, who were always good at answering questions compassionately, so I knew she was in good hands. Years later, Allie said she does not recall that night or discussing that it was probably going to happen. But Anne Grace had no one nearby. I had asked her if she wanted to be in Nashville with us, and she did not. It was a Tuesday, and she had classes and impending exams. I pictured her excuse note, even though in college it is not needed:

Please excuse Anne Grace and allow her to take her exam late. She was in Nashville to attend the execution of a friend.

I hadn't fully pictured what that evening in her dorm would look like.

"I told my friends at school just briefly, so they knew not to talk about it," she said. Then she sent a private Facebook message to her closest friends from church, ironically many of whom were not on the same side of the issue, "Please pray for Cecil and his family and my family," she wrote, "no matter how you feel about it." She and I texted a few times during the evening, and when it was over, I let her know.

"I didn't talk to anyone in person," she recalled. "That was it. I read his poems, three of them that he had sent me." This was probably one of them:

"Father It's Me Again"
Father, it's me again. I want to thank You once more for Your love. As I continue to realize it, I remember all the times when I thought no one cared about me. I have learned that Your love for me will never fall short. That helps me to live my life with true contentment.

Father, it's me again. I say out loud how much better my life is now; knowing of Your love. My eyes see a beauty about life that has been there all the time. My perspective on life has improved immensely; for knowing You're for me each day is a wonderful blessing.

Father, it's me again. I want to witness that my eyes are open now. And things that once held them closed don't blind me anymore. Throughout my mind and heart, I know peace in ways that lifts me far above the things that once kept my spirits down.

Father, it's me again. I realize that you are the only true beginning and the ending of each day. I know that You are the reason why I live each moment. And I know that Your love is more beautiful, more wonderful than anything I have ever seen.

"Then, I read his last letter," Anne Grace adds about the night, "and cried in my bed."

CHAPTER FIFTEEN

WE DIDN'T THINK THEY WOULD REALLY KILL HIM

Minutes Until Execution

ASSOCIATED PRESS REPORTER ERIK SCHELZIG WROTE IN THE *Knoxville News Sentinel*:

> Thirteen minutes after the lethal injection began, Cecil Johnson was officially declared dead at 1:34 a.m. Bob Bell Sr. and [victim James] Moore's brother witnessed the execution in a separate room from Johnson's family, [Department of Corrections Spokesperson Dorinda] Carter said. They did not speak to the media after the execution.
>
> When the blinds to the execution room were lifted, Johnson lay strapped to a gurney with medical tubes strapped to his skin. He mouthed "I love you" to his [family], and was asked whether he had any final words. "You all stay strong, and keep trusting in the Lord," he said.

After the warden said "proceed," daughter Deangela Johnson, 30, turned away and covered her ears as her father took two deep breaths, fell asleep and began to snore. She tried to leave the witness room but was told by a guard that she couldn't until the warden announced the time of death.[1]

Standing in that rainy field, I knew when he died because a feeling of relief and happiness passed over me. I no longer had a friend on death row. And I realized that for the first time in twenty-nine years, Cecil was free.

Cecil had asked his lawyers to witness his death so Jim Thomas and Jim Sanders, who had poured their professional lives into this cause, went to the prison that night to watch the culmination of all that work. Elizabeth Tipping, a lawyer at Neal & Harwell who had helped with the case, was also there, standing outside in the rain. Jim recalled that cell phones were not allowed in the prison, so Elizabeth was outside waiting for a call from the U.S. Supreme Court. When she got the call, she went inside to tell her law partners there was no stay.

"We had filed everything we had to file, pending in the U.S. Supreme Court, a few days before. We were still waiting to hear from the court, literally within the hour of the execution time," Jim Thomas said. "I was starting to wonder what we were going to do if we got to the appointed time and had not heard."

He had not considered *not* attending. "I felt like that was part of seeing it through. It was something I had to do. The other reason I was there was in case something had gone wrong at the last minute." But nothing went wrong; it went according to the plan.

"He appeared to go peacefully. I hope that's true. I was grateful for that."

Add these lawyers to the list of people whose lives were changed: "It's hard to articulate [how it affected me]," Jim said. "It's something I think about every day, one way or another. I continued to carry on after Cecil's execution, but it was a cloud and remains a cloud." He spoke carefully as he thought back to the whole ordeal. "Twenty-seven years is a long time to put into something. It definitely took a toll personally and professionally, to put so much time and effort in and ultimately fail."

In a very long line of people who had failed Cecil throughout his life, Jim Thomas and Jim Sanders did not do that. Jim Thomas may say he failed, but he did not. He and Jim Sanders *showed up.*

At a news conference the day after the execution, Rev. Joe Ingle and others close to Cecil said again that he did not commit the murders. I felt grateful that others were carrying on with that narrative because Alan and I were too exhausted and heartbroken to be in the public eye. This was reported in the *Tennessean*:

> Johnson maintained his innocence for nearly three decades. Joe McGee, a minister who counseled Johnson for many years, said Johnson walked into prison an angry man but later changed and seemed at peace near the end.
>
> "He said, 'If it's God's will, I'm willing,'" McGee said. The Rev. James Thomas, of Jefferson Street Missionary Baptist Church, served as Johnson's spiritual adviser and said Johnson winked at a group of family and friends shortly before he was put to death.
>
> "Death had no power over him," Thomas said.[2]

The media continued to cover the story. Every radio report or newspaper story was a gut punch reminder. I hoped that David,

Deangela, Sarah, and other family members were not also hearing and reading all the accounts, but how could they not?

The sister of one of the murder victims, James Moore, had mixed feelings about the execution, *The Tennessean's* Kate Howard reported:

Her family, scattered across the country for decades, had no idea a date was set. Learning about it opened a very painful old wound. She said her brother was an intelligent man who played classical piano and had a young daughter. "Even though you never forget, you can kind of move on," Betty Hunter said. "You try not to insist on the how and the why, and time has a way of healing all those wounds to some degree. Don't forget, but you do kind of move on."

Moore was the valedictorian of his high school class and studied physics at Tennessee State University, and his family says he grasped concepts so easily that be barely had to study to make the grades they had to work so hard for. But the man known as "Pretty Mo" was more concerned with enjoying each day, surrounded by friends and loved ones, than keeping his nose in the books. "My family has lost the presence of my brother," Hunter said. "If the courts have decided based on the information they received that he's guilty, at least he's lived 29 years longer than my brother. My brother's life was taken for no reason."[3]

When I read that, my heart went out to that sister, as it had for all the members of the victims' families.

In all the reports of the execution, the *Tennessean* included the Hobson service, quoting me and pulling from my *Journal* column.[4] It wasn't long before I received an email from a man who had read the story, too. He asked if during all the time we visited Cecil if we had also visited with any "family members of the twelve-year-old boy that Johnson shot in the head." Noting that the story said I "choked back tears," he wanted to know if I had ever cried for any of the victims' family, or if I had reached out to them at all.

He had good questions. I had not reached out to them.

Although these people had lost loved ones, because I felt that Cecil was wrongly convicted, I did not think of them as having to do with Cecil, as having been *his* victims. Still, I wish I had given more thought to the victims. It was a horrible crime, no matter who did it.

Not wanting to engage this person (who had clearly done some digging to find my email address, which I found unnerving), I didn't answer him. A week later, he wrote again to say it didn't surprise him that he hadn't heard from me.

"Certain questions are just plain hard to answer, aren't they?" he wrote.

After that, I wanted him to know that I had given a lot of thought to his contentions. So, I answered.

Yes, certain questions are hard to answer. You are correct that I do not know the victims' families. But I don't understand how my caring for a human being in prison implies that I don't care for anyone else. I do care about the victims and my heart breaks for them. … You may be right that we should've made time to reach out to all involved but we did not. I hope that someone else, perhaps you, did. If your ministry has been to care for the families of the victims, then thank you—and I'm sure you received a blessing, as we did in ministering to Cecil.

Weeks and weeks passed with no response, so I assumed that that took care of it, but that turned out to be wrong. Two months later he wrote again, thanking me for responding, but standing by his original contention.

The guy was very articulate, quoting Matthew 25 back to me and questioning my interpretation of it. He believed that I had extracted the verse, twisting it for my own purposes. "Go back and read the verse," he wrote. "It says 'to visit.' No less, no more."

That seemed like a narrow way to look at it, but I was starting to understand how he could be outraged at my position. The letter continued, telling me to envision "someone putting a gun to my twelve-year-old child's head and killing him." He had some detailed visuals for me to consider about despicable acts "that only an excuse for a human being would ever do."

The exchange unnerved me for a couple of reasons. First, I was concerned that he knew that we did, in fact, have a twelve-year-old child. Why did he specifically bring that up? Was this a real threat?

Second, he and I were operating on different beliefs—that Cecil was guilty or not guilty. The premise of his angered argument was based on me defending a murderer. But because I believed in Cecil's innocence, I did not feel like I had defended a murderer. (Although, I'm pretty sure Jesus did stand by murderers even when he thought they did it. And it took me a while to understand that innocence shouldn't matter when it came to showing compassion for another human being.)

This man was right about one thing. It was not difficult for me to imagine my outrage and need for retribution if someone caused harm to my child, and I could see that if someone took up for a person who had hurt her, it would anger me beyond reason, too. Maybe he and I were not so different.

CHAPTER SIXTEEN

THEY SHOWED UP

———

TEN DAYS AFTER CECIL DIED, ALAN, ANNE GRACE, ALLIE, AND I walked into the back of the Mt. Calvary Missionary Baptist Church in Nashville a little before 11:30 a.m. Mt. Calvary is constructed of a light-colored brick, the sanctuary shaped from the outside like a triangle, a narrow white steeple shooting from the roofline. We walked through the double doors into the sanctuary not knowing what to expect.

Sarah had asked Alan and me to speak at this memorial service. I'm sure planning it had been a challenge since during these days she, Joe, and Brad were still fighting the medical examiner in court to keep him from performing an autopsy on Cecil's body. My parents were already there, sitting in a pew up on the right-hand side of the center aisle, so we joined them. There were few people on that side but over on the left, many of the pews were filled, and I strained to try and figure out who they all were. Spotting Sarah, we nodded in encouragement.

Right behind us was a man we later met, who had been released from death row in another state. He had not known Cecil but came in solidarity for him and against the process.

We sat quietly and waited as more people filed through the doors and down the center aisle, filling in on both sides. Above us the beams of the angular roofline were exposed, reminding me of praying hands. A stained-glass window shown bright at the front, casting a colorful glow from behind the choir loft and pulpit.

Cecil's dear friend, the Rev. Joe McGee, began, opening with a prayer, followed by the choir singing some hymns. Someone read one of Cecil's poems, "Can You Understand Me?"

If you cannot trust in the Lord,
You will not be able to acknowledge my true heart.
If you do not believe in the word of the Lord,
You will not understand my walk.
If you are always worrying about the troubles in your life,
You will not realize why I smile so often.
If you cannot forgive your brother man,
You will not be able to perceive the love I feel.
If you do not have real faith in the Lord,
You will unequivocally not understand me.
If you allow hatred supremacy in your heart and mind,
You will not comprehend my joy and happiness.
If you cannot completely trust your life in the hands of the Lord,
You will not be able to know peace.
If you cannot put the Lord first in your life,
It will be impossible for you to perceive the concept of my life.
If you worship idols, wealth and fame,
It will be extremely difficult for you to define the life I live.
If you cannot believe in the power of the Lord God,

You have no chance to understanding me.
If you cannot accept the Lord, Jesus Christ as your Savior,
You will never comprehend my faith.
Can you understand me?

Another friend of Cecil's sang a solo and quickly we were down to the portion on the program called "Words of Comfort." The Rev. McGee spoke first and, as the program said, we followed; we were also listed as "ministers." I hoped they didn't think we were actual, ordained ministers because I didn't have a lot of wisdom to impart in that messy situation. The "minister" label made me feel even more like a fraud, someone who certainly shouldn't be trying to help people through this sadness. In fact, during the singing, I was scrambling to figure out what to say.

Once again, I found myself in a church, scribbling notes on a bulletin. This time however, I was revising my speech because it had slowly dawned on me that the packed pews on the left side of the church were likely filled with Cecil's family members. And on the very front was a man who certainly had to be Cecil's father.

The prison "destroys many families—many lives," Cecil had written a few years earlier. "It destroys much love between people, it ends many relationships that are needed, and in many instances, it replaces them with more suffering, anxiety and misery. ... Through many years, I've lost all my siblings and their support in every way."

It became apparent to me that my prepared and practiced speech was not going to work. I had planned to say what Cecil told us many times: we were his family now; that he felt God had seen that his family had abandoned him and sent us instead. But when I looked around that sanctuary and saw everyone, I had to wonder where they had been all those years. But that they were there at the funeral was a wonderful surprise, and for all I knew they could have been writing to him regularly, possibly in recent years, although he had never mentioned that. But now, they showed up, and that counted for a lot.

His father was in the front row. I couldn't look at him, knowing what I knew.

Alan spoke first, focusing on our time with Cecil, the changes he had created in us and our family through his love, humor, and resilience. My steely-eyed and big-hearted husband recalled the many times we left the prison thinking how we had been ministered to more than us ministering to Cecil. Alan said he was glad that he had thanked Cecil for that. After Alan finished speaking, I scooted closer to the microphone, while picturing myself running down the aisle and out the back door. Instead, I spoke, staring over the top of Mr. Johnson. I looked at Cecil's brother, David, and Sarah and tried to smile as I introduced myself to the congregation. I explained how we knew Cecil. I described that last visit we had, the one with David and all the laughter:

We listened as they recalled childhood memories: how everyone is doing, how proud they both were of their kids and grandkids, how much they love their wives.

What struck me was how intent Cecil was on hearing David—and really listening. *He was a good, good listener.* Cecil had some serious matters on his mind—this was less than two weeks ago—but he was only concerned for David at that moment.

Then he turned to us: *How are the girls taking it all? How are you doing?* He was always checking on others. The stories he and David told were funny—and comforting for them to relive together. But they were also stories of survival, where two brothers depended on each other in very harsh situations. I got to thinking about that. Cecil had a rough start in life—as many of you know because you were there, too. And circumstances never really got better for him—in fact they got worse.

At that point, I wanted to wag my finger at Cecil's father and point out what all I knew about certain "harsh situations," but I forced myself to keep my focus toward the back of the room, away from his stare. I also couldn't look to the left where my parents and daughters were sitting. I would have disintegrated had I met their eyes.

On that day I was not open to the idea that Mr. Johnson himself had changed or perhaps regretted things he had done. It was possible. Cecil had changed since his early years before prison and at the beginning of his incarceration. He had told me more than once how being in prison had saved his life because if he had continued down the path that he was on, he would've died sooner. As bad as it was, being in prison gave him time to know himself and others better, and eventually be redeemed. In front of the church, I kept talking:

But by the time *we* met Cecil—although he could not change his surroundings or circumstances—he had changed his heart; *God* had changed his heart. His life was pretty tragic, really, but if I said that to him, he would've laughed that off and started counting the ways he was blessed.

He was one of the most joyful people I've ever known.

I only figured out the words for that recently when the Sunday School lesson we had in my eleventh grade girls' class was about the difference in joy and happiness. It was about

how a person could be joyful even in bad circumstances—
even if they are not happy about what's happening. The girls
were saying how that seemed impossible—and Cecil's face
popped into my head. If anyone ever had a reason to be
unhappy and cranky, it was Cecil Johnson. But he had that
JOY. You know that.

I am just a passable speaker even in good circumstances but
throw in the tiniest bit of emotion and the risk is that I will
choke up to the point where no words can get out. I'd say there
was a tad bit of emotion involved in this, so I dabbed my eyes
with a tissue, ground my back teeth together, and pushed out
each word slowly, one by one. I told how when Alan first started
visiting, I didn't go but that we began talking on the phone.
Cecil had won me over:

Eventually our daughters got to know him and when he would
call, we'd pass the phone around to everyone. We laughed a
lot about random things like fishing or cooking. I always told
him he needed to write a cookbook of all the great recipes he
came up with using odd, wacky prison ingredients. ...
But sometimes after we hung up from talking, it would
strike me that not once during the call had I thought about
where he was. He didn't let that get in his way of feeling and
spreading joy.
He sure didn't let it define him.
In 2 Corinthians 5:6-8, Paul talks about how we are away
from the Lord while we are in *this* body, but when we are out
of this body, we are home with God.
It says: "Therefore we are always confident and know that
as long as we are at home in the body we are away from the
Lord. We live by faith, not by sight. We are confident, I say,

and would prefer to be away from the body and at home with the Lord."

And Jesus' story of Lazarus and the rich man in Luke 16:22-23 indicates that *we are immediately in heaven or hell upon death.*

I have found that to be a comfort.

The night Cecil died I was in a nearby field with a candle in my hand, surrounded by other people with candles. I could see the building where he was. And I watched it. I know from reading these and other scriptures that when he died—the second he died—he was in heaven with Jesus.

So, I watched the clock. And I watched the sky over the building, and eventually I knew that *finally Cecil was free,* and in a place—a home—where he could be comfortable and cared for.

I like what Jesus says in John 14:1–4 to comfort His disciples—only I can't picture the disciples. But I can picture Jesus saying it to Cecil and to us: "Do not let your hearts be troubled. Believe in God; believe also in me. In my Father's house are many dwelling places; if it were not so, would I have told you that I go there to prepare a place for you? And if I go and prepare a place for you, I will come again and take you to myself, so that where I am, there you may be also. And you know the way to the place where I am going."

It was quiet in that sanctuary as Alan and I stepped out from behind the pulpit. My eyes cast down, and we made our way back down the aisle to our seats.

Rev. Joe Ingle got up to speak. He had been through a lot being a friend and spiritual adviser to so many men on death row. He'd seen too much up close. He was broken-hearted for Cecil, for our system that kills people in the name of the government. He was angry, and although it must have been sucking the life out of him to say it aloud, it really helped us to hear. Because we were angry, too. We were angry at the State of Tennessee. We were angry at the legal system and what seemed to be a weak defense that was mounted at trial. We were angry at every person and circumstance along Cecil's journey since July 1980 who did not seek the truth, dig deep enough, or investigate clues that cast an erroneous shadow. And we must admit anger at ourselves for not being aware of it all sooner.

It was a service packed with emotion, for sure, including the eulogy given by the Rev. James "Tex" Thomas. Allie doesn't remember that or anyone else who spoke, what was said, or what the place looked like. But what she does remember is still with her all these years later: it was the sound from across the sanctuary of an eerie pain so profound rising up from someone's heart and guts. She craned to try and see who it was, but she could not, as the deep sadness of the grief-stricken cry ascended and crashed into heaving sobs, blanketing the congregation, expressing how we all felt.

CHAPTER SEVENTEEN

DECIDING WHICH LIVES ARE WORTH SPARING

FINALLY, THE AUTOPSY DISPUTE WAS RESOLVED TWO WEEKS AFTER the execution.[1]

"We ended up winning," Joe Ingle told me, "but it was very strange and convoluted as these things are."

Brad MacLean explained, "We went into federal court where we eventually lost and then we went into state court where we won. In state court, we relied on the recently enacted Tennessee religious freedom act. Ultimately (and quickly) the case went to the Tennessee Court of Appeals, which ruled in our favor." One thing that came out of it is that new precedent for this situation was made. "Basically," Brad said, "the court held that if a condemned inmate has a genuine religious objection to being autopsied, then generally the state cannot autopsy him after the execution."

Sarah was finally allowed to claim Cecil's body, and have it flown to Las Vegas, where she lives, and he is now buried.

A few days after the execution, Alan brought the annual State Employee Holiday Party invitation home, an event hosted by the governor and first lady, as they had done every year since Alan began working for the state. This time, the invitation lay on the kitchen table like it might sear a hole in the tile. The party had become a staple of our December festivities going back to when we needed to ask my parents to babysit the girls while we went. The girls could stay by themselves now, but the party was scheduled not too long after that other government-sponsored event, Cecil's execution.

I recalled the holiday festivities from past years, especially the first time we were invited. That night, we were checked through security to proceed up the winding drive to the governor's residence. We got in line to greet and have our picture taken with the governor and first lady by the official state photographer. Happy to see them, we froze our smiles for the photographer as we stood at the base of the cascading grand staircase. A heated tent was near the back patio where lavish food and drink awaited. In another room, a band played, and Alan and I danced and danced.

Over the next six years, while the house was being renovated, the holiday gathering was held at the Tennessee Tower (where the first lady's and Alan's offices were located in downtown Nashville), the Capitol building, and finally, back at the Executive Residence, this time in the underground structure associated with the house's renovation, Conservation Hall. Alan had been integral in all aspects of that major project, and I got the best tour of anyone, as he showed me every detail, including the corridor steps made from reclaimed logs found in the

Tennessee River and the oval glass panel rising from the front yard that opened into a light-filled garden area below.

These parties always included very important people— the attorney general, various senators and representatives and Supreme Court justices, who I knew through my work. But these were social occasions, and we only talked about the lovely view or how delicious the canapes were. The first lady always asked about our girls by name, keeping up with them through the years. She was genuine, and I always enjoyed seeing her.

I usually love irony, but when I saw the 2009 invitation and pictured the receiving line to the governor and the small talk with him and other government officials, I thought, *you know what? I'm just going to have to sit this one out.*

Nine months later, in August 2010, an assistant to the first lady contacted me. They were going to give a special, surprise luncheon to thank Alan for all he had done on her two big projects. The first lady wanted to make sure it was scheduled before Anne Grace went back to college, so she could attend. She also invited my parents; she realized that Alan's mother was too sick in the nursing home with Alzheimer's to be able to attend. Mike Fitts, who had retired as state architect, planned to be there as well as others who had worked closely on these projects.

The girls, my dad, and I arrived at the residence early, parking in a place Alan would not see when he arrived. (Unfortunately, my mother had a prior out-of-town commitment.) We walked up the brick circle drive, approaching the Georgian two-story structure that Alan had worked to help restore, a multi-year project that he had thrown his heart into and enjoyed so much. Referred to by many as the Governor's Mansion, it isn't really a mansion, although it is imposing and stately. Knowing that decades of different governors and their families had lived there reinforced its thick air of history. As we climbed the stone steps, the front door swung open, and we were welcomed in as if we were family coming to Easter Sunday dinner. We were ushered into the formal dining room.

Alan had been summoned under the guise of needing to tend to some detail on the residence, although that part of his job was largely finished. He was rushing from downtown and called the guard house and asked them to tell the first lady, he would be a little late.

"She's here and waiting," the security officer said.

"I felt terrible I was late for her—and then worse later when I realized all those people were waiting on me," Alan later said. "She had it all planned out—had me meet her in front of Conservation Hall, so I wouldn't see all the cars." She told him she needed to show him something in the residence, so they rode the elevator from the underground hall up to the house. "She was walking in front of me, and I heard people, but there were always people around in there." Then, he turned the corner and saw his girls, his good friend Mike, the governor, and me. "I was genuinely surprised," he said.

After the hugs, the handshakes, and an official photograph with the governor and first lady at the foot of the grand staircase, we were directed to the table where we saw place cards with our names. I found myself seated at the governor's left hand. He was at the head of the table, and Alan sat across from me, the girls next to him. The glittering chandelier hung high over the elegantly laid table, a fireplace behind them.

I had not seen the governor since before the events of December 2, 2009, and I was nervous. He had a lot of concerns, the death penalty being one among many, and I didn't know if he had even ever connected us with Cecil Johnson. I wondered if he had read my letter for clemency, or if the first lady had told him about her conversation with Alan.

This luncheon was just days after a historic event in the state—the governor had granted clemency to Gaile Owens, a woman on death row (who the following year, as it happened, was released). I was happy for this woman, who had confessed to hiring a man to kill her husband years earlier, but who had changed in prison and had become a model prisoner helping others. Also, there were many issues not brought up in her trial, such as a history of abuse from her husband. The similarities of her and Cecil's conduct in prison seemed obvious to me. But there were two big differences: she was white and a woman; Cecil was Black and a man. Also, she admitted her crime, and Cecil maintained innocence, although convicted.

At any rate, Cecil's execution was all I was thinking about, and I could barely focus on the red-ripe tomatoes and fresh mozzarella caprese salad in front of me. Inside my head, I was screaming, *ASK HIM. Ask him if he got your letter, if he had waivered at all, or if he even remembers Cecil's name.*

Had we been characters in a novel or a movie, I probably would've clinked my crystal stemware with a knife to get everyone's attention, stood up, and grilled the governor, causing awkwardness and embarrassment for all. But I am enough of a Southern Lady to know not to cause a scene, not to steal someone else's day. I had taken the "White Gloves and Party Manners" class as a girl and knew how to behave in polite society.

So, when I heard myself murmur, "Thank you for what you did for Gaile Owens," I stunned even myself. Was it my imagination or did both my girls jerk their heads up in fear, knowing what I must've *wanted* to say to this governor, concerned over what I might say next? But the low din of polite conversation around the table did not stop. He looked me in the eye, holding his fork and knife over his plate.

"Well," he said, "it was the right thing to do."

I held his stare, searching his eyes for any flicker of recognition as to what this might mean to me, to our family, if he had noticed that he gave leniency to a white woman, but not a Black man. I *know* that there were hundreds of differences, circumstances, and details that set those two cases apart. But I wanted to ask if he read my letter, studied the incongruous details of Cecil's case, or what his thinking was on changing Cecil's sentence to life from death; why wasn't that also the right thing to do?

But I only said, *Mmmhmm*, and we went back to our salads, as I speculated silently how if one life was worth sparing, why not the other? How did he weigh all the factors?

Statistics bear out that more Black men are executed in this country[2]—it's a complicated mesh of bias, both intended and unintended, coupled with poor legal representation for those who can't afford it. And then there is the fact that most of the people making the decisions—police, judges, jury—are white, and bring, at best, an unintentional bias, and at worst, active racism. But that was not the time to take that up with the Governor. I reached for my crystal goblet of iced tea, wondering how he drew that fine line between the worth of the lives of Gaile Owens and Cecil Johnson.

Cecil had not worried about things like that, was not petty, and would've been happy that Gaile Owens had been released. He clearly was not a grudge-holder. Eight or nine years earlier he had written:

There was many sleepless nights where I stared into the darkness, asking why me. I repeatedly wondered how they can get away with this. … I felt myself falling into despair, yet I knew that I had to climb back up. I got out of bed, kneeled and begun to pray and pray again. That very same night, I wrote a poem called "DEAR GOD." Once I was finished writing that poem, I no longer felt despair's hand in my life. Day after day I learned to put my troubles in the hands of the Lord. Though I had to understand that the lord answer's our prayers when He is ready and not when we feel we need them answered.

"DEAR GOD"

Dear God, please incline Thine Ear to me. This world that I live in is painted with loneliness, sorrow and pain. Nearly every day loneliness comes and touches my life. Often my thoughts remind me of all the things that once enlightened my life with happiness, peace, laughter and love.

Dear God, please help me in my plight. Instill in me a bit of your wisdom so that I may possess strong insight and integrity. Bless me with new strength, so that I can endure the many empty moments in my life. Day after day I see the same discouraging picture, my face without a true smile.

Dear God, please lift Thy Hand, lift it to help me survive in a world of darkened days. With Thy Hand I cannot fail nor will I be discouraged to walk further in life. With thy Hand I have the ability to stand strong, to survive through anything.

Dear God, please send an Angel to me. In my life I live in a world of woe—a place where adversity dwells continuously. With an Angel from Thy heavens, I will not be destroyed by troubled times. I will strive diligently and not yield to the devastating life I'm forced to encounter and endure.

Dear God, please enlighten me with new knowledge and virtues, so that I may survive through a world of destruction and oppression. Instill in me the ability to stay focused when bleak times fall heavy on me. Bless me with strong endurance, because in this world I live the darkest days of life.

That day at the Tennessee governor's residence had not been the first time my dad had been with a governor in an official capacity, and even though the governor likely wasn't thinking about recent capital cases at that luncheon, it surely was on my dad's mind that day.

A couple of decades earlier, he had stood in North Carolina's Capitol Rotunda, lights from TV cameras shining in his face and microphones poised. It was 1984 in Raleigh, and he was about to assure the good citizens of North Carolina through the media that Gov. James B. Hunt had no plans to stop the execution of James William Hutchins. Hutchins would become the first person to be executed in North Carolina since 1977 when the death penalty was reinstated in the U.S.[3]

My dad worked for Hunt as Citizen's Advocate, but the job also now encompassed dealing with the extraneous fallout from carrying out two death sentences within the same year. Dad's heart was not in this defense of the governor's stance, but he and the governor had known where each of them stood when he took the job in 1979.

The governor's position was that he was elected to carry out the laws of the state—and the death penalty was the law. Instead of leaving in protest from this job, however, Dad stayed in the face of this uncomfortable position, using his ministerial training and innate compassion to help where he could.

On that night at the Capitol, the victims' families wanted assurance from a state official that the execution would be carried out. They felt that an execution would avenge the death of their loved ones and would soothe their grief. A representative of the governor—an ordained Southern Baptist minister fully opposed to the death penalty—was who they got. They would've been able to see his minister's concern, but because of the job he was hired to do, his personal views on capital punishment were not part of the discussion.

Later that night, I picked up the phone at my apartment in Nashville, ten hours away from my parents in North Carolina, for our weekly call.

"Your dad was on the news tonight," Mom said. This wasn't that unusual, since his job was kind of high profile.

"Why?" I asked, only half listening.

"He caught a distraught woman as she fainted in the Capitol."

"Was it you?" I said, hoping I had made a joke. She explained how a victim's family member was about to make a statement to the media about the execution but was overcome with emotion and passed out. This was a reminder of how hard and emotional the execution process is for everyone, no matter which side you are on.

Once again, I had not been paying enough attention. At the time, I didn't know that four years earlier, in the same city where I now lived, Cecil Johnson had been accused, tried, and sentenced to death for murder. Even if I had known it, I would not have thought it had anything to do with me.

Later in 1984 in North Carolina, Velma Barfield held the dubious distinction of being the first woman to be executed in the United States after the reinstatement of the death penalty, and the first since 1962.[4] Because of the changes she had made in herself while in prison, including helping young inmates acclimate and even helping stop a prison riot, many people had asked for the governor to spare her life. The warden even pled for Velma's life, explaining how much help she was with the other prisoners, quelling violence, and helping young women adjust to prison life. Even that had no effect.

My dad did not know about Cecil then, but he knew this fifty-two-year-old woman, Velma. Just one year older than he was, they were on different ends of the situation, to be sure. Years later he told me about that night and the events leading up to it. And hearing this, I realized that watching my dad in this situation helped prepare me for what to do once we did meet Cecil.

On the scheduled night of her execution, Velma was denied a stay by the Fourth Circuit Court in Richmond, Virginia, and had been denied stays from the U.S. Supreme Court three times. It finally sunk in to everyone that it was going to happen. Dad was invited inside the women's prison hospital where the authorities had allowed Velma's incarcerated friends to gather to watch the news reports and share their grief. He was introduced as a minister friend of the chaplain—his association with the governor's office was disguised, except to the assistant warden and officials. They feared he would be in danger from the inmates if his true connection were known. But he was not there in an official capacity at that moment—he was there as a minister, showing up, full of compassion and sadness.

A couple who had visited Velma for the previous fifteen years had just been with her for the last time, and they told the group about pressing their hands up to Velma's through the glass, singing and praying with her. Everyone was crying by this time.

Later, and back in his official capacity, my dad went with the chaplain to address a room full of corrections officers and prison employees. It's easy to forget that an execution takes a toll on those who have to carry it out, too.

"I spoke in a very quiet voice as to how much I appreciated their long hours and professional work," he told me. "As I shared feelings of how they were the unsung heroes and unrecognized as very important people, there were nods and smiles of approval. They were clearly astonished that a representative of the governor's office was there."

As he left the prison, driving slowly by, he saw an eerie sight. "Those for capital punishment were on the right side of the highway being interviewed by TV," he said, "and on the left candles burned in the hands of those against capital punishment. Cars were backed up on the side of the road from a half mile with the green lights casting a carnival atmosphere over the scene."

Television reports that night said there were five hundred people outside of the prison, about two hundred of them members of the press from all over the world. In the end, no amount of improvement to her life or for others—clear by all testimonies, Dad said—made any difference.

"The facts that she was abused as a child, raped by her father and drug-laden during the time she committed the crime were not in the court record—but that didn't make much difference," he said. "The letter of the law was carried out."

About six years before he was involved with the two North Carolina executions, Dad had received a telephone call from the Rev. Will Campbell, whom he had met through his work at the Christian Life Commission, the social action agency of the Southern Baptist Convention in Nashville. At that time, Dad was the director of public relations. Will was involved in organizing a march against the death penalty to be held in Atlanta. It was in protest to what seemed to be the looming possibility of a rush for more executions after the 1976 *Gregg v. Georgia* decision, which had reinstated capital punishment in the United States.[5]

The march would go through downtown Atlanta and end on the Capitol steps. Former attorney general Ramsey Clark, journalist Tom Wicker, the Rev. Joe Ingle of Tennessee, and other civil rights proponents agreed to speak at the march, but Will wanted to add a pastor of a large church in a mainstream denomination.

"Floyd," Will had said, "I need you to find me a big steeple preacher to speak at this march." Will could not find a prominent member of the clergy from a large church to agree to come and publicly speak out against the death penalty, so, after failing to find a high-profile pastor, he asked my Dad to come. He lined up my college-age brother, who was a pilot, to fly him down there. (Note that this was 1978 when the SBC would have supported this effort to save a condemned person's life, pointing out that Jesus would not have been in favor of killing anyone and that it does not solve anything. The Christian Life Commission is now defunct; and this position would likely not be supported by the SBC today.)

"That's as close as I've come to being a big steeple preacher," Dad chuckled. He noted that in 2015 when the execution of Kelly Gissendaner in Georgia came into the news, many "big steeple preachers" signed the petition to stop it, although she was ultimately executed.

"The mood has changed a little since the '70s," he said.

CHAPTER EIGHTEEN

IT WAS TIME WE KNEW

"I DIDN'T WANT TO FOCUS ON THE CRIME," ALAN SAID, SOME YEARS after the execution. "I wanted to focus on Cecil." His reasons are better than mine: I didn't focus on the crime because I didn't want it to get in the way of our friendship. If I knew more, would I even have been able to continue to support him? This thought jolted me, as I began to wonder if my support had been contingent on his being innocent. I don't *think* so, although let's be honest, that makes it easier. But the whole point of compassion is that it is given freely, because a human being deserves empathy and concern, regardless of guilt or innocence. That's a tough one, though.

What little Alan and I knew about the crimes we had learned at that one hearing we attended back in 1995, and then nothing else until the time of the execution. In 2009, news reports recounted all of his crimes in great detail, once the execution date was set. I still did not want to know, but I couldn't avoid the headlines appearing in all the papers and news reporters talking about the upcoming execution on television and radio. The murders, for which Cecil was convicted, were reported a lot in the news in Nashville when they had happened, and there was renewed interest in the original trial and outcome.

As the execution approached, the media's stories rehashed every reported detail of the crime and trial. At first, I averted my eyes when I saw the headlines, but soon people were asking me, "Is this the guy you visit?" and talking about what they had learned in the paper or on TV. I realized it was no longer serving me well to keep my head in the sand. I didn't want to know less than the general population.

It was time I knew, and I let myself read all about it.

That's when I learned about Cecil's convictions for murder, assault, and armed robbery. The sentences were death and four consecutive life terms.[1]

In 2009, Kate Howard wrote an article for the *Tennessean* quoting a previous interview with Cecil from a *Nashville Banner* article in 1980. That article was written three weeks after his arrest:

Johnson said he felt like he was stuck in a bad dream. He said he met with police after hearing they were looking for him and told them he was in Franklin with friends at the time of the slayings. He told the paper that he and Victor Davis were just driving around on a pretty summer day, looking for women and dice games, not for the massacre that happened a few blocks from his dad's home.

He was surprised when he was arrested and denied bond. "I feel like this whole thing is wrong," he said.

But the witnesses said otherwise.[2]

It is astonishing to me that his word and Victor Davis's original account did not count for much. Howard described the night of the crime this way:

Bobby Bell Jr. was crying hard as he filled a sack with money and gave it to the gunman. He and his father, Bob Bell Sr., were inseparable, and on that hot Saturday night in July 1980 the boy was working the register at his father's store. The 12-year-old sold Cokes and snacks while the elder Bell and his friend worked on a motor. They were about to close for the night when a man burst in with a six-shot revolver.

Although he did everything the robber told him to do, Bobby was shot point-blank in the head in front of his father.

…

When the man walked into the market with a gun in his hand, Louis Smith didn't realize the gravity. He said he thought the man and Bell were "just jiving," until he was ordered behind the counter.

Minutes later the shooting started. "I jumped on the child," Smith testified. "I didn't think he'd been shot yet."

But a bullet had struck little Bobby in the head. Smith was shot, too. As the man pointed the gun at the head of Bell Sr., he threw his arm up in defense. His wrist stopped the bullet. "Did anyone do anything to provoke the shooting that you know of?" then-prosecutor Tom Shriver asked Smith on the stand. "No. Bob begged him to try to keep him from it," Smith said.

On his way out the door, the man fired two shots, and prosecutors theorized they were the last two bullets in a six-shot revolver. James Moore, a Nashville native and Army veteran who had just started driving for Supreme Cab, was behind the wheel of the taxi. Moore and passenger Charles House died inside the cab.

Bell counted quickly to 10 and jumped up to get his shotgun at the back of the store. He tried to chase the man out, hearing the shots that were fired into the cab as he ran. He told a reporter later that he couldn't have fired the gun anyway, with the bullet in his arm. He stood helpless outside.

Bell said he knew Johnson as a customer in the store who sometimes wore clothing from Vanderbilt. Bell didn't know his name but said he knew the face.

"I think (Bell) has made a mistake that he doesn't want to back off of," Johnson told reporters shortly after his arrest. "He looked straight at me and said, it was me. Everything inside me fell down. ... I don't think he was lying. I just think he made a mistake."[3]

What Cecil did not know at the time, which I learned from reading appellate court documents[4] decades later—and his own lawyers didn't even know for twelve years after the crime—is that one of the main witnesses who told police on the night of the shooting that he did not see the assailant's face, later chose the pictures of two *other* young Black males from a set of lineup photos. Once he did identify Cecil from a lineup, he admitted later that he had already seen his face on TV during his arrest. Another witness, who said he looked the robber in the face, identified the culprit as having no facial hair, yet in Cecil's mug shot, taken within hours, he has a mustache and goatee. There were several other inconsistencies regarding the eyewitnesses, much of which was not available to Cecil's trial lawyer at the time it was needed most.

The *Tennessean* story continued:

After Johnson was convicted, his attorneys asked the jury to consider his youth and lack of serious criminal history before sentencing him to death.

Johnson testified at his trial that he was never at the market. But Bell, Smith and two other witnesses identified him as the shooter. There was no physical evidence linking him to the scene, and the murder weapon was never found. But four witnesses testified that Johnson was the killer—one of whom was planning to be his alibi witness, until he was arrested himself a week before trial.

The next day, after an interrogation by the district attorney's office and a promise of immunity, Victor Davis was a witness for the state. He testified that he dropped Johnson off at a car wash just before 10 p.m. when the murders happened. Johnson told him he was going in to rob Bob Bell and said he didn't intend to leave any witnesses. He said he sat with him later at Johnson's father's house as they counted the money, and Johnson gave him $40.[5]

Davis was the only person who told that story. The money was never found, and Cecil's father had not mentioned if Cecil and Victor were at his house counting money. (Cecil later said in an appellate filing that he had given his father some money, but it was from gambling winnings.) I could not stop reading this newspaper story. When I came to the part about the unusual witness identification, it was one more in a string of shadows cast on the case. The story continued:

The district attorney who led the interrogation, Sterling Gray, was later appointed to a judgeship and indicted on charges that he took bribes from defendants in exchange for light sentences. Gray killed his wife and himself that same year. Jim Sledge, an investigator with the district attorney's office who worked on the case, said Gray himself was not the only person involved in that interview. He and the other prosecutors were there, too, he said, and it was above board.[6]

What was never disputed though, once it was discovered, was that the prosecutors withheld evidence. The district attorney admitted it, and it still made no difference. The *Tennessean* story continues:

Johnson's attorneys raised the flipped witness as well as questions about the eyewitness testimony in their appeals. Several police reports saying that Bell's friend Louis Smith never got a good look at the accuser were withheld from the defense attorneys, and it wasn't until 1992 that attorneys for Johnson learned of their existence. The district attorneys admitted that the reports were withheld and that the information could have aided Johnson in his defense.

But the federal appeals court ruled the mistake didn't affect the outcome of the trial. Smith admitted that he identified Johnson after seeing him on television, already arrested in the murders, but denied that was the reason he picked him. A panel of federal appeals judges ruled 2-1 to deny Johnson's appeal. In a scathing dissent, Judge R. Guy Cole, Jr. wrote that the jury "saw a markedly different trial than it would have" if the prosecutors hadn't withheld the reports.

"Because 'fairness' cannot be stretched to the point of calling this a fair trial, I dissent," Cole wrote.[7]

This is a serious problem. A dozen years after the crime, prosecutors admit they didn't share everything they knew. That's when Cecil and his attorneys finally had all the pieces to the same puzzle the prosecutors had all along. In that 2008 dissent to the decision issued by the United States Court of Appeals for the 6th Circuit, Judge Cole couldn't have been clearer that there were omissions, missteps, and suppression of evidence—in his dissent the judge focused on six items withheld that he strongly believed could have changed the outcome of the trial. Specifically:

> Johnson's case is not even a close one. ... Confidence that Johnson's verdict would have been the same simply cannot survive a recap of the suppressed evidence and its significance for the prosecution. The withheld evidence, taken together, reveals at a minimum that one witness's first and most lucid description of the assailant did not comport with his in-court identification, that one witness may not have [been in the] store on the night of the crimes, and that one witness implicated someone other than Johnson when confronted with a photo array containing Johnson's picture. These were the same three witnesses that the Supreme Court of Tennessee called Johnson's "insurmountable problem."[8]

Judge Cole continued:

> Had the prosecution disclosed the six items of withheld evidence, competent defense counsel may very well have destroyed the value of their identifications, or at least raised serious questions in the jurors' minds as to their reliability. This is to say nothing of the potential inferences of police and prosecutorial misconduct that the jurors may also rationally have made had they been apprised of the suppressed evidence. Simply put, Johnson's defense was substantially crippled in cross-examining the three critical witnesses on the only serious issue in this case—identification.[9]

Cecil was fighting for his life in this trial, and he and his lawyers were not even working with all the information? And the "insurmountable problem" of the witnesses' identifications appears to not sound all that insurmountable to Judge Cole. This judge was laying out all the trial lawyer had to do to refute the pieces of the prosecutor's case.

"The entire case against Johnson consisted of only four witnesses and no physical evidence," Judge Cole wrote. "One of the four witnesses was originally scheduled as an alibi witness to corroborate Johnson's innocence. On the day before trial, after a coerced midnight encounter with the State prosecutor, that witness flipped. As for the other three witnesses, the State admits that the prosecution withheld evidence that would have impeached each witness' identification of Johnson as the perpetrator. To say the least, the jury saw a markedly different trial than it would have had the prosecution honored its Brady obligations."[10]

Judge Cole, who is Black, was just one judge of three on the appeals panel. The other two—Judges Alice M. Batchelder and Julia Smith Gibbons, both white women—were equally as convinced that the evidence withheld would not have changed the outcome of the trial had Cecil's lawyers had access to it. I can appreciate their point of view. But it is more than troubling that a person can be executed with this kind of reasonable dissent, doubt, and unanswered questions on the table.

Even with the other two judges' apparent certainty, it seems as if Judge Cole's clear reasoning of these problematic issues would give the court pause. How could it come to pass that death was still the only answer? Why at this stage can there not be a clause like, "Well, we're two-thirds confident he did it and that it's been fair, but geez there sure are a lot of murky parts so let's not kill the guy just yet. How about we keep him locked up and look into it some more."

But that's not how it's set up. Once a person has been sentenced to death, even if the playing field is uneven, even if there is an admitted unfairness, it seems to be nearly impossible to change course.

CHAPTER NINETEEN

MORE PUZZLE PIECES

WE ALMOST NEVER GET TO LEARN WHAT IS GOING ON INSIDE A person's thoughts. So when I read Cecil's account of his trial, it meant more to me than all the other angles. Like his description of his arrest—I believe what he wrote about his trial. These are some specific details and emotions:

> [My trial day] was a day I had been looking forward to, I was ready to leave and show the people that they had the wrong person. I had all sorts of plans on suing them. ... By this time, I have a new lawyer. [Note: This was Mike Engle, after his father had dismissed the public defender, Walter Kurtz.] My father had hired him, but this was his first big case such as mine came to be. He told me that no matter what is said true or false, it is best for me if I remain calm and no outburst. So I did just as he suggested, the next day the newspaper read, "MR JOHNSON SHOWED NO EMOTION. JUST A COLD

STARE." I couldn't believe what I read. Several time it was very very difficult for me to sit there and not protest some of the false things that was being said about me. During the process of picking a jury for me, they said that they was picking a jury of peers. I kept thinking to myself, I'm in my twenties, so how could the people that were much-much older be my peers. I couldn't believe all the things the District Attorney was getting away with. He was calling me names that anyone who knew me, knew that they wasn't my name. One in particular was the name "ICEMAN." I told my lawyer many times about things that was untrue, but he did nothing about it and on most occasions he would try to quell me with a gesturing nod. I was absolutely stunned when I found out that Victor Davis was suddenly testifying for the District Attorney. Then I found out that he had been arrested for several crimes and were threaten to be charged with the crime they were trying to put on me. I stared at him as he sit on the witness stand hoping he would look in my eye, but not one time would he look at me.

Then some woman gets on the witness and says she know it was me, because she went to school with my brother James. I tried to tell my lawyer that this woman had me mistaken with someone else. It didn't matter what I said because my lawyer had no proof and they believed her. I knew that I had never seen this woman every in my life and I never attended a high school named Overton. When nothing was done to correct all the false testimonies, I felt so wronged. Still my lawyer wanted me to remain calm, for it was my time to get on the witness stand. I thought now I can straighten all this out, but before I could leave for the witness stand, my lawyer told me not to say anything other then the answer to the District Attorney's questions. Reason because he is clever enough to use it against you. He was right how he would twist things up, they had went and gotten some of my clothes and brought them to the courtroom. One a garment I had on when I got hit in the head at the pool hall, it had my blood on it from where I got hit in my head. If I knew he was going to bring that, it could have been properly examined and they would have found that it was my blood and that it was a little over a year old. There were so many things that my lawyer could straighten out if he had knowledge about them bringing such things to my trial. My lawyer rebutted was weak because he was not prepare for all the things the District Attorney had presented. If he had known about it all, he never said anything to me about it. If he had I could have helped him greatly.

… I will never forget the District Attorney's closing argument, because he pretend he was horrifyingly afraid of me everytime he allowed himself to get close to me. What a show he put on for the jury, it was truly expressive. The deliberation didn't take long and before the jury came back in, the judge said that he didn't want any outburst or trouble after the verdict is read. When they said they found me guilty, I wanted to scream out I'm innocents, but I had to remain quiet. As the feeling of "this isn't right" flooded my soul, I looked over and I could see my mother crying. I felt right then that this was the worse day of my life.

As I left I thought that they were going to kill me soon, because I didn't know anything about the law. … They took me directly to the Prison [and] once I saw the prison in the shadow of darkness, it looked like a large castle from a horror movie. … As I walk through the doors, all eyes were turning to me. Suddenly I felt numb as I walked forward. … All I could think about is that I was sentence to death for something I didn't do. I went to sleep with only that on my mind. It was still very difficult for me to believe that I was on Death Row.

It all pointed back to the trial. Had that been handled differently, the appeals process might not have even been necessary, and Cecil might not have been sent to death row.

"It was a true travesty of justice," appeals lawyer Jim Thomas told me later. "Totally unfair trial. In our post-conviction petition we made a big issue that Mike [the original trial lawyer] didn't move for a continuance. He should have. He had ample grounds for a continuance after that change. Victor Davis went from being a defense witness to being a prosecution witness, in a case without a lot of witnesses. That was in our [appeals case] papers repeatedly."

Jim Thomas kept track of Victor Davis's whereabouts "until the bitter end," trying to find out more. "But he wouldn't talk to us," he said.

In a later appeal, the 6th Circuit had found that his lawyers, Mike Engle and Robert Smith, had "not been ineffective," which I thought was a pretty weak thumbs-up. But that ruling allowed plans for the execution to move forward. I had not looked into who they were because I was pretty sure that I would hate them.

But once again, I learned that things are not always how they appear at first. When I talked with Mr. Smith years later, he told me this about the post-conviction hearing: "Mike and I freely agreed to all contentions of ineffective assistance of counsel. However, the judge found that our efforts at trial were not so, and that our testimony, and I am kind of paraphrasing, was in effect the consequence of remorse and to benefit our client."

Even more than the others involved in Cecil's case, it was very personal for Mr. Smith. It turned out they had grown up in the same neighborhood, on the next street over from his parents' house, and he had frequented the store where the incident took place. "During the course of representing Cecil, we became good friends," he said. "This was a difficult case." He distinctly remembers the emotional impact of the trial on the family when he visited Cecil's family's home to prepare them for possible testimony at the penalty phase hearing, where they reacted with anger and fear.

"I have not forgotten Cecil," Mr. Smith told me decades later. I can only imagine his specific pain as Cecil's case worked its way toward execution.

Riding the elevator up to the twentieth floor of the Parkway Towers Building to the Davidson County Public Defender's Office, I was again regretting my decision to know more about Cecil's case. In particular, I was feeling some distress that I had contacted Mike Engle to ask him more about it. I was on my way to interview him, and I was nervous. This was about five years after we had first met at the church service, the night of Cecil's execution.

The waiting room reminded me what the situation was for most of the people who came there. They could not afford to pay for a lawyer, true, and they probably had little idea how the system worked. A very professional-looking place, the reception area was sprinkled with clients waiting patiently, some of them with children who were playing in one corner full of brightly colored toys.

Mike greeted me, and we went on a tour of the floors that made up the Public Defender's Office, ending in his corner office with glass on two sides, a stunning view below.

Dressed in khaki pants and a denim shirt with a tie, and reared back in his chair, Mike put his feet up on the desk and began his story.

When Mr. Johnson, Cecil's father, came to see him after Cecil had been arrested, Mike had been in private practice about six months. At thirty-six years old, Mike had spent some years in the Public Defender's Office right out of the University of Tennessee College of Law before he set up his own firm. His own new law office at that time was in sight of his former workplace and also the old Davidson County jail.

Cecil's trial was assigned to Judge Adolpho A. Birch, who later would be appointed to the Tennessee Supreme Court, and who died in 2011 at the age of seventy-eight. He was the first Black person to serve as chief justice in the state.

Looking out the window of Mike's office, I could see the relatively new legal complex—the Justice A. A. Birch Building with all its courtrooms, judges' chambers, and jail cells—and the Cumberland River's wide brown smudge winding past.

Mike said Mr. Johnson came to see him because of Judge Birch's requirement to get a letter of rejection from an attorney. Later Birch stopped that practice, Mike said, but on that day when the Johnsons needed representation that was how it was. So, Mr. Johnson went to see Mike, probably because he knew him since Mike had represented Cecil on that prior aggravated assault case when Mike was still a public defender.

"I do wish I had not taken that case," he said, shaking his head slowly as if he's still baffled as to why he had agreed, all these years later. "I'm not sure why I did." He said he knew that it would have been better if the Public Defender's Office had been appointed. Walter Kurtz was the public defender who was first assigned to Cecil in the first hours after his arrest.

Even Walter Kurtz agreed. "It became apparent to Mike that he didn't have the resources." Kurtz is now a retired Circuit Court judge who has presided over four death penalty cases himself. In the early 1980s, he was a public defender in Davidson County.

"Mike asked if we would get back in the case. He asked the judge if we could be appointed second chair or co-counsel, because we had the resources, and he didn't." Kurtz remembers being in court when Engle asked about appointing his office as backup. "I said yes, we would undertake to do that, but the judge said no."

Instead, Judge Birch appointed Robert L. Smith, a young Black man who had only been out of Howard University School of Law about four years at the time. Smith also had his own private practice and therefore was in a similar boat as Mike, as far as having limited resources and time.

"He's a good guy and hardworking," Kurtz said of Smith, "but he had no experience. You can only speculate why the judge did what he did."

After reading Cecil's memoir and knowing what I did about how his father treated him and others, for the first time I could see that Mr. Johnson must've wanted the best for his son at the time of his arrest. I mentioned my surprise to Mike that Mr. Johnson seems to have been there for Cecil, even after the horrifying childhood he helped create for Cecil.

Mike, who didn't know much about Cecil's childhood, pointed out that "the case was tried before people had an appreciation for mitigating factors," like child abuse.

I looked down at the cityscape below us, took a deep breath, and decided that while we're there I'd ask the big question.

"Do you think he was innocent?"

"I think I may be one of the very few people who believes that," he said, taking his feet off the desk and leaning forward. "For a death penalty attorney, that's the worst possible position for an attorney to take. But you gotta believe. Experts on the death penalty talk about totally conceding guilt and factoring mitigation into the guilt phase of the trial and not deluding yourself that your client might not be guilty."

Mike has represented three people in capital cases that went to trial and verdict, but Cecil is the only one of those who has been executed. Knowing a former client was ultimately executed was painful I was sure, but I wondered if Mike's belief of Cecil's innocence made a difference twenty-eight years later.

"It is significant," he said, "and it makes it hurt more." There were others who were "very opposed to his being executed" as well, he said.

Mike had believed Cecil was innocent twelve years before all the information had even been shared by the prosecutor with Cecil's defense. This "new" evidence was something that Jim Sanders and Jim Thomas asked about when they took over the appeals representation.

"From the beginning of our involvement in the case we'd been pursuing potentially exculpatory evidence," Thomas said. "The state always said there wasn't anything." [During that time there was a Court of Appeals decision that expanded the scope of the Open Records Act in Tennessee. This allowed them to request the information, some years in.] "So, we decided to take a run at it under the Tennessee Open Records Act. The problem was that once we got the exculpatory evidence under the Act, we then had to start all over again, so that set us back several years in effect, to the point that by the time we were finally able to get into federal court, the federal habeas law had changed to our disadvantage. The good news was, we got the ruling [for the exculpatory evidence]; but the bad news was, it created at delay that was fatal to Cecil's case."

Jim said he was "disappointed and surprised. I felt very strongly that we ought to get a new trial. After the change in the federal habeas corpus law, I knew the deck was stacked. But I remained optimistic that we would ultimately prevail because we had such a strong case."

These are legal maneuvers that take time, drug out further by the evidence that was withheld. All I can think about, though, is every single day that added up to years while Cecil sat in that cell as these things were slowly, slowly being dealt with. I could picture it because he had written about it some years earlier:

During countless quiet moments, I have agonized over the feelings and thoughts on what I have lost—what I am still losing. Every night as I close my eyes in this unseen world, I face the indisputable fact that I will be facing it and enduring it all again for another day. This comes along with the realization that I lost more than just another day.

Each new day in here is a sure bet that more misfortune than goodness is in store. ... The darkness of night is my silent world away from the world in which I reside, where no one knows my pains or sees the anguish and torment on my face.

Although Mike no longer represented Cecil, he told me Jim Thomas called to tell him when the withheld evidence was discovered.

"It didn't surprise me," he said with resignation. Knowing all of this, it made more sense that Mike would've shown up at that church service the night of the execution. "I went out of loyalty to a former client." He also told me that he went to the candlelight vigil later that evening, and although I was also there, I had not noticed him.

"I do believe in rites of passage," he said about why he went to the services. "There ought to be times that you acknowledge that life is transitioning. It was important to be there for that, and with people of similar thinking or who knew him. It was reaffirmational to my beliefs that this was totally wrong, unjust and a violation of what I believe." He also wanted to be at that last gathering in case there was a reprieve for Cecil.

"There is always a hope that magic would happen in the Sixth Circuit," Mike said, "although that's pretty rare."

Hal Hardin is an authoritative and esteemed lawyer in Nashville. He is a former United States attorney for the Middle District of Tennessee and served as a circuit judge, the presiding trial judge in Nashville, and, for a few cases, a special judge on the Tennessee Court of Appeals. He is a former president of the National Association of Former United States Attorneys, an organization composed of former federal prosecutors. He earned his law degree from Vanderbilt University Law School.

In November 2009, with just weeks before the scheduled execution, Cecil's lawyers at Neal & Harwell asked Hal for his expert opinion on the issue "involving the state's failure to provide exculpatory evidence to the defense" in this case. Exculpatory evidence is any evidence, whether admissible or not, that may reflect on the guilt or innocence of the accused at trial or impacts sentencing. Not all exculpatory evidence rises to the level of being material, Hardin explained in a letter to Jim Thomas, dated November 16, 2009:

> In other words if the evidence would have made no difference in the outcome of the case, the verdict normally stands. Clearly exculpatory evidence must be turned over by the prosecutor even in the absence of a request by the defense. Once a request has been made for exculpatory evidence, prosecutors cannot take the attitude that 'it is not in my file.' … It is his or her affirmative obligation to look for it. Since at least 1963, prosecutors have been warned by many Courts to err on the side of disclosure. … Good prosecutors do that. In summary, as I told my criminal procedure students and staff for years, this is not a complicated law, it involves basic human fairness, something that your parents should have taught you by kindergarten.[1]

Hal was not on the fence at all about whether he thought the missing evidence made a difference in the outcome of Cecil's trial. In the letter, he could not have been clearer that it was unfair—and had all the evidence been available at the time of the trial, he believes Cecil would not have been found guilty and certainly not sentenced to death.

This was eye-opening to me, as another piece of the puzzle snapped into place. Hal's letter continued, detailing the questions that must be answered regarding the facts.[2] Among them, he asks if the evidence would "most probably have affected the outcome of the trial. Yes. It is doubtful to believe that any honest experienced trial lawyer would doubt that."

Regarding eyewitness identification, Hal did not mince words:

Contrary to popular belief, [it] is some of the weakest evidence one can have at trial. That fact has been established by the Courts and researched extensively. The damning evidence in this case was the eyewitness identification of witnesses. If the jury had known that these two witnesses had given conflicting statements, indeed contradictory statements, one would have to conclude that a good, law-abiding juror would give great weight to the conflicting statements. This would be especially true since the contradictory statements by the eyewitnesses were made immediately after the crime than their later statements. Such contemporary statements are known to be much more valuable than statements made at later dates.

The question of where the exculpatory evidence was found was the most shocking to me. *Had it been lost? Was it misplaced, and the prosecution didn't realize it was available?* No. Hal continued:

It was found in the prosecutor's own file. While the good faith or the bad faith of a prosecutor in failing to turn over exculpatory evidence is normally not a controlling issue, denial of due process is the same regardless of a prosecutor's good faith or lack thereof. Occasionally, police officers fail to turn over statements to the prosecutor. However, this is no excuse. It is the ethical and legal duty of a prosecutor to look through his or her own file and also the file of all agents who were involved in the case.

In this case, the exculpatory evidence that should have been turned over was found in the District Attorney's own file. One would have to conclusively assume that any District Attorney would go through his or her own file prior to the trying of the lawsuit, especially this high-profile lawsuit. I believe that the second and third chair prosecutors most probably did not go through every paper. The lead prosecutor most certainly would have done that.

Allow me to venture one other observation. No jury has ever seen this evidence. *While no one can predict with certainty what a jury will do, I believe if you asked one hundred good trial lawyers whether they would feel that with this evidence a defense verdict would be likely, I believe most would say yes.* [Emphasis added.][3]

The team of prosecutors at the original trial was District Attorney General Thomas H. Shriver, Victor S. (Torry) Johnson, and Sterling Gray. Mike Engle said he "would've dealt with Torry on discovery," which is the part of a legal action where the lawyers find out every available thing they need to know about the facts in order to put their case together.

"Torry had the basic organizational point and pretrial processes" in this case, Mike said, but Shriver had "a heavy finger in investigation and argument. Sterling's role was partially in argument." Shriver, now deceased, was white; Johnson is white; Gray, now deceased, was Black.

For Shriver, Mike said, it was a "very rare court appearance." He didn't often try a case, he said, but was personally involved in this one. "He had a reputation of rarely seeking the death penalty."

Shriver gave the opening statement, and Torry Johnson gave the closing. Shriver's statement was later found to have been improper, according to the 6th Circuit. Cecil's attorneys had contended that Shriver "inflamed the passions of the jury by improperly using inflammatory language and injecting statements of personal interest into his closing argument." The court agreed, noting:

In his closing rebuttal argument, Shriver told the jury:

I have a very personal interest in this case, and I suppose that is why I am here today. Little Bob Bell, twelve years old, started out in the first grade at Burton School with my twelve-year-old daughter. They started, they have gone through school together. Burton School, Stokes School, would have gone to John Trotwood Moore together this year. It could have been my little girl that was in that store, a witness eliminated. It could have been you. It could have been your children. It could have been any one of us, if we decided that we wanted to buy something from Bob Bell, at nine fifty-eight on July 5, 1980, we would have been dead.[4]

Shriver was Davidson County District Attorney from 1966 until 1987 when he became a judge in Criminal Court, Division 1, where he served until his death in 1997. As D.A., Shriver hired the first Black prosecutor in the South—who was none other than Adolpho A. Birch,[5] the judge who several years later presided over Cecil's case where Shriver was the lead prosecutor. Although apparently no one raised an objection to it, Birch's old boss, Tom Shriver, was the lead prosecutor in the trial Judge Birch presided over, the one that determined the fate of Cecil's life.

That seems unusual, I thought. You would think that a judge who had previously been hired by the man who now was one of the attorneys appearing before him in this serious case might recuse himself from overseeing that case. Or that the District Attorney who hired that judge years prior might stand aside from the case. Or that Cecil's lawyers might raise an objection.

But Jim Thomas, Cecil's appellate lawyer, told me years later that it's very common for assistant district attorneys to become judges. "It's a common career path. So there was nothing unusual about that, and it's not a basis for recusal." After Shriver was appointed judge, Torry Johnson followed in his footsteps and became Davidson County District Attorney. He was re-elected to three additional eight-year terms, retiring in 2014. He then became a visiting professor at Belmont University's College of Law, where his areas of expertise are listed as criminal law, criminal procedure, and prosecution ethics.

Torry Johnson is a well-respected lawyer, having served in leadership positions with the National District Attorneys Association and the Tennessee District Attorneys General Conference. According to Belmont's website, he has been a part of task forces and commissions dealing with various topics of criminal law and sentencing. Over the years, he has been recognized with awards for his contributions to victims' issues and to the legal profession.[6]

Since he is the only one of the three prosecutors in Cecil's case who is still living, I asked him about the evidence that turned up only many years later. This is what he wrote to me in an email:

> As I am sure you are aware, all appeals and federal habeas litigation is handled by the Attorney General's office, often with little input from the trial attorneys. In cases of this type, defense attorneys invariably make allegations of "prosecutorial misconduct" and are often seeking to apply evolving standards to cases that were tried decades ago, just like this one. There were three attorneys for the state in this case and I have no recollection at this time about any material that was or was not provided at the trial. In fact, I don't recall whether I was ever interviewed by the defense, and I definitely never testified in federal court. Obviously the federal court found the omissions not to have been material to the defense since the attorneys were able to cross examine all the witnesses extensively. Beyond that, I can't add anything to the discussion.[7]

A federal court did recognize that evidence was withheld. The reason that didn't slam the brakes on the execution was because two judges on a three-judge panel then ruled that it would not have made a difference had Cecil's lawyer been working with all the information that the prosecutors were privy to. Whether or not it really would have made a difference, we will never know. But it is not disputed that the evidence was withheld.

"It is fundamental and firmly established that a defendant's due process rights are violated," Judge Cole wrote in his dissent, "where the government (1) withholds evidence (2) favorable to the defendant (3) that is 'material either to guilt or to punishment.' ... The State concedes that it withheld favorable evidence that would have assisted in Johnson's defense. At issue is only whether the suppressed evidence was material."[8]

"I can't say for a fact that Torry knew what was there," Jim Thomas said years later. "I do remember he fought us about it until the law was so clear that he didn't have anything to fight with anymore. Mike [Engle] made all the appropriate requests but they stonewalled him. The prosecution, under *Brady v. Maryland*, had an absolute obligation to turn it over—and they just didn't." Thomas shook his head slowly. "I was angry and disappointed in the prosecutors, who fought us on disclosing the evidence as long as they could."

"Over our careers," Torry Johnson continued in his letter to me, "General Shriver and I both were cautious in seeking the death penalty, but it was clearly called for in this case."[9]

What the death penalty should be reserved for was a matter of debate, according to Walter Kurtz, who had been Cecil's original public defender, before Mr. Johnson hired Mike Engle instead. "That case came along in the early days of the death penalty. Some of the people who were getting the death penalty were like nervous junkies. [People who] shot the cashier in convenience store robbery for which the death penalty was never intended to be applied." And yet, the death penalty was sought in this case.

The *Tennessean* covered the days leading up to the execution, and the reporter asked about that: "Was this the type of case that was intended to apply to the death penalty?" Kate Howard asked.

"It was a case that captured people's imaginations," Torry Johnson had responded. "Certainly, we had robberies before this, and market owners and clerks were killed. But having a child killed was something that really did make this different. It was shocking to people."[10]

Lawyers provide legal representation *pro bono*—for free—a lot. They take on cases that range from very short in duration with little complications to cases that may take years, requiring expensive expertise and long hours. Taking on a capital case is on the far end of the spectrum, not only needing extensive hours and resources, but with the added pressure that a person's life literally depends on it. Not only did I believe the lack of resources, expertise, and time ultimately hurt Cecil's case, I discovered the personal toll that was suffered by his first lawyer, Mike Engle.

"It cost me my private practice," he said, explaining how a case of this magnitude takes every resource, every second of every day. "You shut down. Or you can try to build the practice at cost to the previous representation." He described his serious cash flow problems and that he went into too much debt. In 1983, he packed up his dreams, folded the practice, and went to work for the state Department of Health. "I was a great person to go to [while in private practice] because if you didn't have the money to pay a fee, I'd take a promise of payment, and then I'd never see it."

Walter Kurtz, the former public defender, confirmed Mike's predicament. "A sole practitioner—it wouldn't matter who— taking a case like that is just one hell of a burden," he said. Even though a lawyer can request some resources from the court, "it's a professional burden, [and] a psychological burden to carry. He's an extraordinary person. He's been in the trenches for a long, long time. There are many other people who slave in the criminal justice system like Mike that don't get the credit they are due. They do one heck of a job. And never get a public pat on the back."

"It did cost me a personal relationship," Mike said. "Someone I was in love with ... [the case] moved us in different directions. Death penalty trials are expensive on interpersonal relationships."

As I listened to Walter after having talked with Mike, I saw one more truth that Cecil's story had taught me: I had judged Mike and Robert without knowing everything; they had tried hard. "Mike was an excellent lawyer whom I admired for his commitment to justice and the underserved members of our community," Robert said.

"He gave everything he had. [That case] was his life," Walter said of Mike. "It had a big effect on him. For Mike to win that case he would've really had to pull a rabbit out of a hat."

For all the "big effect" it had on Mike Engle and others involved in the case, it is safe to say that the consequences of everyone's actions affected Cecil the most, ultimately resulting in his death. These puzzle pieces are only clear to me in retrospect, but every part of the system contributed to the ultimate outcome:

- from the poor decision Mr. Johnson made to choose an inexperienced solo practitioner over a better-resourced, experienced public defender
- to the decision Mike Engle made to take the case
- to the jury not hearing any mitigating evidence like that of Cecil's abusive childhood, or the discrepancy that an eyewitness claimed the assailant had no facial hair, but Cecil's mug shot shows he had a mustache and goatee
- to the jury not hearing about an eyewitness who had said he did not get a good look at the assailant, then chose *two different people, who were not Cecil*, from a lineup; and ultimately choosing him after seeing Cecil's face on TV at his arrest
- to the decision or omission the prosecutors apparently made to not provide all available evidence to the defense until forced, twelve years after trial
- to Cecil's friend and alibi, Victor Davis, changing his story right before trial to implicate Cecil in exchange for

immunity, and several surprise witnesses at trial for which the defense was not prepared—and that Cecil's lawyer then did not ask for a continuance to allow for his defense to regroup when Davis upended his defense at the last minute, and the trial went on

- to the narrow decision of the Sixth Circuit panel including a scathing, heartfelt dissent by one judge saying the original trial had not been fair; to the many other denials and decisions.

Like a ripple in a pond, these events and others kept Cecil in prison for twenty-nine years, away from his family, until he was executed. And although we loved him like a brother by the end, guilty or innocent, it was not until I put all these fragments together that I believed that Cecil surely was innocent of the crimes for which he paid.

CHAPTER TWENTY

THOU SHALL NOT KILL— NO ASTERISK

THIS PROCESS AND THE TOLL IT TOOK WAS HARD TO WATCH. BUT our family was only fifteen years in, and Cecil had been dealing with the case for twenty-nine years—as well as figuring out and reconciling unfair, painful things his entire life. After years of being in prison and learning about writing and poetry, he was able to describe the journey well on paper:

I have come a long way and learned much. … Studying the Scriptures and trusting the Lord helped change my life day by day. The anger that once ruled my emotions daily abated. I have read the entire Bible twice now and if someone would have told me that one day I will enjoy studying my Bible I would have thought them crazy. Often I find myself going back to study the book of Job. It compels me to look inside myself

*and at the same time it increases and strengthens my faith. It
modifies my perspective on life and all the pain I've endured
become insignificant, less painful. Today many people wondered why I am so strong. It isn't because of me; all praises go
to the Lord. ... I have wisdom, my heart is whole and I know
the peace within myself. ... I know not to worry about things
that are out of my control.*

*Most times when people see me smile it's difficult to com-
prehend due to my predicament. With faith and trust in the
Lord comes my joy and peace. Today I walk a new walk, I
don't need drugs to feel good about who I am. In the Lord's
eyes I know that all His Children are special in some way. ... I
don't need to be wealthy to enjoy the goodness of life. The Lord
promises to take care of me and have so from the beginning of
my life.*

"I had seen something no one else had seen," Anne Grace
said, that people who have not been this close to a situation
"can't possibly think the way that I do." She, like me, can't
understand the reasoning behind the death penalty, except for
vengeance. And I do understand revenge. She acknowledges
that it would be the normal first response to want retribution
and that she has not been in their shoes, so she doesn't know
what that would be like. This is a feeling our family shares.

Perhaps, she has been most surprised that often the people
who are determined to get revenge in hopes of easing their own
pain, use the Bible for justification. I asked her why she thinks
victims' families and others push for death, and she took a
breath before speaking.

"I would ask if they were a believer [in Jesus Christ]," she says
of death penalty supporters. "Because if they weren't, I would
get that. They wouldn't have the understanding [of Jesus's

forgiveness] to go off of. My bigger problem is with people who say they are Christians who do that."

She recounted a lecture given at her university by Sister Helen Prejean, a mighty opponent of capital punishment. Anne Grace noticed, by the questions members of the crowd asked, that many of the people there did not seem to have religious motives.

"When they said why they were there, it wasn't faith-based; it was because [inmates on death row] are people too and the system is not fair. It didn't seem like saving them [religiously] was their main purpose," she said, starting to tear up. This was a new angle for her to hear, and it helped open her understanding. The unfairness of the system is enough to question the situation, but from her perspective of a lifelong churchgoer where Jesus and forgiveness were part of every lesson, she saw the disconnect of fellow Christians when it comes to capital punishment.

"Why aren't people who *are* believers out there also caring—and carrying out the Commandment, 'Thou shall not kill'?" She was full-on crying, and I wanted to shout, "*Preach!*" as she continued, but I stayed quiet.

"Why are you limiting God's power by giving up on them?" she asked the phantoms in the room. "You are saying 'God, you're not big enough to save these people.' Saul killed thousands of people; then he wrote the greater part of the New Testament. We look to him as being a great teacher, but he was once killing people."

I looked at my wise little girl and reached back for the tissue box.

Considering second chances, salvation, and timing, I recalled a recent conversation with my life-long friend, Mandy. I had told her about Cecil as we were walking in the park. Mandy is a physician, a profession that has trained her to keep people from dying, first and foremost.

"Who am I to deny a person's opportunity to find God in the time remaining of their life?" she wondered. "If they don't find God, it is on them. And what if the state killed them right before that happened? And who am I to repeat the same act as the convicted murderer?"

She was not comfortable with anyone, including the government, choosing when a life will end, for that reason alone.

And there is the unlevel playing field, the disproportionate number of poor and Black men sent to death row. According to the Death Penalty Information Center, jurors in Washington state are three times more likely to recommend a death sentence for a black defendant than for a white defendant in a similar case. In North Carolina, a study found that the odds of receiving a death sentence rose by 3.5 times among those defendants whose victims were white. And in ninety-six percent of states where there have been reviews of race and the death penalty, there was a pattern of either race-of-victim or race-of-defendant discrimination, or both.[1]

None of that gives the impression that the death penalty is being applied fairly or evenly. In fact, up close it seems a little bit random.

"The system is riddled with arbitrariness," wrote Bradley MacLean and H. E. Miller Jr. "When over the past forty years Tennessee has executed fewer than one out of every 400 defendants (less than ¼ of one percent) convicted of first-degree murder, when Tennessee sentences ninety percent of multiple murderers to life or life without parole and only ten percent to death; when the majority of capital cases are reversed or vacated because of trial error; when the courts have found that in over twenty-three percent of capital cases, defense counsel's performance was constitutionally deficient ... then it must also be said that the death penalty is an 'unusual' and unfair punishment."

They continue: "The lack of proportionality and rationality in our selection of the few we decide to kill is breathtakingly indifferent to fairness."[2]

Furman v. Georgia,[3] the 1972 U.S. Supreme Court case that invalidated death as a punishment, if only for a few years, explains: "The penalty of death differs from all other forms of punishment, not in degree but in kind. It is unique in its total irrevocability. It is unique in its rejection of its rehabilitation of the convict as a basic purpose of criminal justice. And it is unique, finally, in its absolute renunciation of all that is embodied in our concept of humanity."

These are some of the injustices and arbitrary applications our family began to see up close as Cecil's friend. And the harsh details of Cecil's childhood, which did not get into the record at his trial, remind us that he started and ended this life at a serious disadvantage.

"The Bible says, 'Thou shall not kill,'" Anne Grace continued. "It doesn't have an asterisk at the bottom that says, 'unless *they* have.'" She has since graduated with undergraduate and graduate degrees in Social Work. Learning about Cecil's childhood and the terrible situations he endured informed her decision to go into that helping field. One area she is interested in is the prison system or other related areas, which cannot be a coincidence. During her training and early jobs, she saw many childhood situations like Cecil's and wondered, *had someone been there to help him, would things have turned out differently for him*?

The thing about social work is that pretty much every area is full of people's hurts. Some have been shocked at this prospect, a beautiful young woman putting herself in such an undesirable profession. You can see it on their faces.

"Ah! Every mother's dream," an acquaintance recently said sarcastically to me about Anne Grace's thought to someday work with the prison population. And although I don't relish the idea of her being in a prison setting, frankly, it *is* this mother's dream to see her drawn to such an ugly, shattering profession, one in which she will patch some hurts, bring some kindnesses, and strive for justice.

My father has told Anne Grace that he sees that it's not just a college major but that she is *called* to this ministry, this thing called "social work." *Of course, it is a calling*, I think, *because who would do it otherwise? It's too heartbreaking.*

"I feel like no one else wants those people," she said, her hands rearranging the used-up tissue. "Sometimes I feel like I'm the only one who does, and it's my obligation."

"Why do you say you don't believe he committed the crime?" A family friend asked about the book that I'm writing where I say, in preface, that I believe Cecil was wrongly convicted. Anne Grace and I were sitting in our friend's living room. She was not challenging me angrily as some have, but she was curious. At that time it had been four years since the execution and I realized I didn't have actual, real evidence in hand to support the claim. Our conversation took place before I read the court documents and saw how the puzzle pieces didn't quite fit, and that a reasonable person—even someone who the man didn't call "little sister"—might see there was room for doubt about his guilt.

You would think that even the slightest bit of room for doubt would keep the government from ending someone's life, but that is not true.

Cecil maintained his innocence in court the entire time, and a reading of related documents—detailing the inconsistent, changing testimony of the eyewitnesses, the lack of integrity with the lineups, the complete absence of physical evidence, police reports that were concealed and took years to be turned over to Cecil's attorneys, and other things that didn't add up— left open *the possibility* for me to believe he did not commit these crimes. That the courts were willing to end a person's life with that kind of uncertainty and muddiness was baffling—and appalling.

But I never asked Cecil, "Did you do it?"

I had plenty of opportunities but never asked, I told our friend. It would've felt harsh and wrong to ask such a thing. You don't question your friends like that. Our family had stuck by Joe Ingle's and Harmon Wray's original advice to not discuss the case with Cecil, and we did hold out until close to the end. We started out with the uncomplicated belief that a person's humanity should be valued, and that person—guilty or innocent, incarcerated or not—deserved compassion. Then, as we got to know Cecil as he maintained his innocence, we began to believe him and were eventually convinced by the disjointed facts.

We had an understanding that we believed the same thing, that he was wrongly accused and that eventually, somehow, that would be proven, and he would be exonerated. That was a relatively new realization for me: at that time, I didn't know exactly *why* I believed in his innocence, but I did.

I looked over to Anne Grace, who was staring ahead, not looking at our friend or me.

"The person you knew was not the same person who may or may not have committed that crime anyway," our friend said, realizing how much Cecil must have changed during his time in prison.

"Right," Anne Grace said. "The thing is that it wouldn't have made a difference." It didn't change how she saw him, guilty or not. Beginning with the innocence of a child, she did what Joe and Harmon (and not incidentally, Jesus) had told us to do. That had been easy for Anne Grace to do from the first time she met him when she was four years old—and the same for Allie, from birth. Just like that: trust and love. It took me a lot longer to come to that nonjudgmental love. Cecil probably had to get used to me, too, now that I think about it.

But once he connected with our family he didn't let go, didn't waiver in his love for each of us, even when we let him down time and again. The things he asked of us were so minor— from Sara Lee Cherry Cheesecake to trying to get his story and poems published—but what he gave us was a deeper understanding of another, unfortunate, and harsh world. We also got to see an unworldly strength, grace, and love that he exhibited every single day.

Nothing I have, nothing I can do without the Lord. I end this book with love and peace, with the smile the Lord has given me.

Like he did us, we cared for him like family and didn't judge him. He was part of our lives and family conversation until that day when he wasn't. The sadness of that will be with us always, but we'll also always have his example of what redemption and love in the face of tragedy looks like.

By the time we might have wondered about details of proving his innocence, we already loved him, this child of God, with whatever baggage he came with.

And that's exactly how he loved us, too.

ACKNOWLEDGMENTS

THIS IS A DIFFICULT SUBJECT TO WRITE ABOUT AND IT HAS BEEN wrenching, but not without silver linings because of all the people who have been a part of it.

For trusting me with his own memoir some years before his death, and for trusting our family to let us into his life, Cecil C. Johnson Jr. is the heart of this story. He asked me in 2005 to try and get his memoir published. I didn't say no, but I sure didn't think it was probable at the time. I didn't start for years after his death; it was so painful. But a little voice kept pecking at me (and I know this was Cecil) to get to it, then stick with it, and to persevere in the face of many, many rejections. I did not give up. In one of his letters in this book, he tells me that I am brave to speak out. I am very often the opposite of brave, but I have taken courage from watching him and other family members during these years. When I got the word from Milton Brasher-Cunningham that Church Publishing Inc. wanted to publish this book, I danced around and cried, and I promise you I could hear Cecil laughing up in the heavens.

Milton is the editor of the century and I adore him. As much as I have had a long-term vision for this story, he somehow jumped in and knew exactly what reorganization and details my draft needed. I have been an editor myself for many years and I could not have been more thrilled to have an editor who would dedicate himself to my work with such heart. Thank you so much, Milton, and others at CPI: Ryan Masteller, Deirdre Morrissey, Anita Manbodh, Anne Zaccardelli, Airié Stuart, Dana Knowles, and Philip Marino. Dana and Philip stepped in mid-production to put finishing touches on the manuscript and see it through, which I appreciated. Thanks to Kathleen Crenshaw for sharp copyediting. For legal review and vetting, there's no one better than Carolyn Schurr Levin, and thank you to Paul Soupiset for the dramatic cover design.

Milton would never have even seen this manuscript had it not been for my dear friend and best-selling author, Dr. Joy Jordan-Lake, who passed it on to him. She has been a champion for this story. Thank you, Joy, for believing in it enough to share it, and for being my sounding board and sister for all things literary.

Dr. Kelly J. Baker was developmental editor on earlier versions and made a huge impact on how I saw it all, asking piercing questions about race and privilege, and pointing out all those unexplored differences between Cecil and me. She knocked out my own blind spots, questioning with kindness and encouragement. She changed the soul of this book and set it on its right path. For putting me in touch with her, I am grateful to the women at Blue Crow Press, who saw potential in an earlier manuscript and directed me to Kelly.

When my friend Mandy Ryden went with me to hear Sister Helen Prejean speak at a book signing many years ago, she stood with me as I very nervously asked Sister Helen if she would look at my book proposal and help me get the story published. She just smiled and told me to keep working at it, that it would take perseverance. But she also said I could contact her once I had a publisher. She flipped to the back of my copy of *The Death of Innocents* and wrote her personal email address. I don't know if I'm more surprised that she remembered her promise after all those years, or that I was able to lay hands on that book with the address when I needed it. But I was ecstatic when she answered me promptly when I asked her to write the Foreword and said, "Let's do this!"

Cecil's wife, Sarah Johnson, his brother David Johnson, and daughter Deangela Nicole Johnson Dunlap, and Cecil's two grandchildren, are all honored here. I hope this account is a tribute to Cecil's memory in the best possible way. He was an amazing person and loved each one of you more than anything.

Thank you to those who walked with us on this journey: the Rev. Joe Ingle, and the late Harmon Wray, who with Joe, got us involved in the first place; our dear, forever friends at Nashville's Glendale Baptist Church; the Rev. Stacy Rector, Executive Director of Tennesseans for Alternatives to the Death Penalty, who walked along side us; Melinda Medlin; best-selling author and friend of my dad, the late John Edgerton, who not long before he died, talked to me on the phone for thirty minutes about the potential marketability for such a book (prospects were terrible, he pointed out, but he encouraged me anyway).

So many people talked with me and opened up through interviews or provided me with documents, statements, and permissions. I appreciate the contributions each of you made: Sarah Johnson, Hal Hardin, Victor S. "Torry" Johnson, Joe Ingle, Mike Engle, Brad MacLean, Ed Miller, the Hon. Walter Kurtz, Laura Click, James G. Thomas of Neal & Harwell, Erik Schelzig, Scott Stroud, and David Plazas.

Thank you to the volunteers at the Family Reconciliation Center in Nashville, who took care of Sarah in the most terrible of days.

Thank you to my longtime writing mentor and author Charlotte Rains Dixon, whose class about nonfiction query letters led me for the first time, to think maybe I could tackle this story about Cecil. Her support through the years has been a bright light to me. Being connected to her by Roy Burkhead was one of the luckiest, best things to happen to me. Thank you, Roy. He started the brilliant writing program at Middle Tennessee State University, at the time called The Writer's Loft, and has led me to so many great writing experiences.

Toward the end of finishing this book, I earned a Master of Arts in Writing from the Naslund-Mann Graduate School of Writing at Spalding University in Louisville. Although I was primarily studying fiction there, the experience and support helped in all ways. The writing community I collected there is so important to me and my process: Kathleen Driskell, Karen Mann, Katy Yocom, Ellyn Lichvar, Lynnell Edwards, Renee Culver, Angela Jackson-Brown, Crystal Wilkinson, Kirby Gann, Erin Keane, Roy Hoffman, and all those in every Workshop. A special shout-out to Terry Price, who never gave up on pushing the idea that I might be able to, someday, go back to school and earn this degree and write.

In 2021, *He Called Me Sister* was awarded second place in the Mayborn Literary Nonfiction Manuscript Competition. This gave me a needed push to continue with the project, even as I was about to stick it in a folder and try to forget about it. Thank you to the Mayborn at the University of North Texas for that and for a long-ago workshop with an early version of this story.

I wish my Uncle Gene Craig could see this book. I would thank him for, so many years ago, asking thoughtful, deep questions in a caring way about our relationship with Cecil, even though I suspect he aligned more with the death penalty than against. I don't know that for sure, but he was a person who could set aside preconceived notions and ideology to drill down to what mattered to another person. When he talked to you, he focused right in on your eyes in the kindest way and was not distracted. He listened so well. That's how we all should talk to each other, although I've never been good at that. Our whole family misses him terribly.

Thank you to these faithful encouragers, who have helped me in ways they don't even realize: Dr. Jason and Elizabeth Rogers, Dr. Robbie Pinter, Dr. Liz Waggener, Dr. Dianne Oliver, Dr. Todd Lake and Dr. Joy Jordan-Lake, Judith and Bill Moyers, Dr. Mandy Ryden, Julie Hancock Armistead, Phyllis Childs, Todd Stutts, Sam Nugent, Lynn Dabney, Carol Bryson, Brad Werner, and Bobby Boyde. Also, Tom Moroney at Bloomberg News; Bill Haltom, who never stops writing or cheering me on; Kathryn Reed Edge, for an early read with a lawyer's critical eye; the Rev. Tambi Swiney, a good friend who invited us to speak on this topic at not one, but two, Southern Baptist churches, a daunting task that was met with more grace than I expected; our dear St. Paul's Episcopal Church in Franklin, Tennessee; Barry Kolar, who helped with some technical details, and the rest of my friends and colleagues at the Tennessee Bar Association, especially the Communications Team; and my girlfriends, the Beach Mamas, who share a love that does not agree on all the issues, but is steadfast, inexplicable, and forever.

My parents, Anne and Floyd Craig, have supported my dreams always, and are the most encouraging people in this world. I am fortunate to have had such an upbringing and I don't take it for granted. Reading Cecil's account of his childhood helped me realize this even more. Thanks, Mom and Dad!

Our daughters, Anne Grace Robertson Werner and Allie Robertson, are intertwined in Cecil's story, and to them I owe so much for being in this experience with us. I worried too late in the process that we had put them in the middle of such a sad, desolate circumstance, but they have each absorbed what they saw, and grown into such compassionate, strong, and caring people. These two have been the center of my world for a long time, and I am so proud to be their mom.

But most of all, this book and the experiences we had with Cecil, would not be in existence without my husband Alan Robertson, who shows us every day what unconditional love is. He has willed this book into being, first by living it through example, and second by supporting me in every way to get it written and published. Thank you, Sweetheart. This is a hard subject to write about and to undertake such a thing, it is crucial to have someone next to you who understands. I have loved and admired this boy for quite a few decades and plan on quite a few more.

NOTES

Prologue

1. *Struggles, Endeavors, Triumphs*, memoir by Cecil C. Johnson II, written in 2005 and given to the author to find a publisher for it. The memoir and reprinted poems are copyright Cecil C. Johnson II and used with permission.

Chapter One

1. Joe and Harmon's presentation for Visitation on Death Row (VODR) took place at Glendale Baptist Church in Nashville, sometime in 1994. VODR began in 1975, as part of the Southern Prison Ministry, which had arisen years earlier through the Committee of Southern Churchmen, with the Rev. Will D. Campbell and Tony Dunbar instrumental in it. Learn more from *Last Rights: 13 Fatal Encounters with the State's Justice*, by Rev. Joseph B. Ingle, 2008.

2. *The Inferno: A Southern Morality Tale*, by Rev. Joseph B. Ingle, 2012.

3. Gregory Boyle, *Tattoos on the Heart: The Power of Boundless Compassion*, Free Press/A Division of Simon & Schuster, 2010.

Chapter Two

1. James G. Thomas and James F. Sanders from the law firm of Neal & Harwell took up Cecil's case in November 1982. In a June 8, 2009, affidavit

where he outlines the steps of Cecil's representation, Mr. Thomas wrote, "a group of Nashville criminal defense lawyers who were concerned about the way that Cecil Johnson's case had been handled approached my partner, James F. Sanders, in the fall of 1982 to ask him to participate in Cecil Johnson's representation on a going-forward basis. My firm has continuously represented Cecil Johnson since that time, both in state and post-conviction and, subsequently, federal habeas corpus proceedings, entirely on a pro bono basis."

Chapter Six

1. Read an enlightening take on forgiveness in *Why Jesus Makes Me Nervous: Ten Alarming Words of Faith*, by Joy Jordan-Lake, Paraclete Press, 2007.

2. Tennessee Innocence Project, https://innocenceproject.org/pervis-payne-wrongful-conviction-what-to-know-innocent-tennessee. At the time of this writing, Pervis Payne remained incarcerated, awaiting resentencing. He is represented by Kelley Henry of the Federal Public Defender's Office.

3. *Brady v. Maryland* (U.S. 1963) held that a prosecutor under the Fifth and Fourteenth amendments has a duty to disclose favorable evidence to defendants upon request, if the evidence is "material" to either guilt or punishment. "Prosecutorial misconduct, either through deliberate Brady violations or the knowing use of perjured testimony or inflammatory arguments before a jury, is designed to deprive a defendant of a fair and impartial trial, and this unethical behavior must be understood and ever guarded against." See https://supreme.justia.com/cases/federal/us/373/83/. Specific to Tennessee, see the Tennessee Board of Professional Responsibility's "Formal Ethics Opinion 2017-F-163, Prosecutors' Ethical Obligations to Disclose Information at http://www.tbpr.org/ethic_opinions/2017-f-163-prosecutors-ethical-obligations-to-disclose-information; and Tennessee Rules of Professional Conduct, Rule 3.8 (d) Special Responsibilities of a Prosecutor.

4. Death Penalty Information Center, "Facts About the Death Penalty: Innocence," updated June 24, 2022, https://documents.deathpenaltyinfo.org/pdf/FactSheet.pdf.

5. "If not for love and art, Ndume Olatushani would have died on Death Row," by Laura Hutson, *Nashville Scene*, May 23, 2013, http://www

.nashvillescene.com/nashville/if-not-for-love-and-art-ndume-olatushani
-would-have-died-on-death-row/Content?oid=3406836.

Chapter Nine

1. *Brady v. Maryland* (U.S. 1963) held that a prosecutor under the Fifth and Fourteenth Amendments has a duty to disclose favorable evidence to defendants upon request, if the evidence is "material" to either guilt or punishment. See https://supreme.justia.com/cases/federal/us/373/83.

2. Order Setting Execution Date for Cecil C. Johnson Jr., July 21, 2009:
On May 26, 2009, the State filed a Motion to Set Execution Date for Cecil C. Johnson, Jr. The motion stated that Johnson had completed the standard three-tier appeals process and that an execution date should therefore be set under Tennessee Supreme Court Rule 12.4(A). On June 8, 2009, Cecil C. Johnson, Jr., filed a Response to Motion to Set Execution Date. The Response contends that the Motion should be denied because the excessive delay in carrying out the capital sentence and the arbitrariness and capriciousness of the sentence in Mr. Johnson's case violate the Eighth Amendment to the United States Constitution and Article I, §16 of the Tennessee Constitution. The Response also asserts that concerns about the reliability of eyewitness testimony expressed in *State v. Copeland*, 226 S.W.3d 287 (Tenn. 2007), require that the Court "reach back" and grant Mr. Johnson's Rule 11 application denied by the Court on October 5, 1998, to review the Brady issue presented by that case. For all of these reasons, Mr. Johnson asserts that this Court should either re-sentence him to life imprisonment or grant the Rule 11 application that it denied in October 1998.

Having considered the Motion to Set Execution Date and the Response, the Court declines to re-sentence Mr. Johnson to life imprisonment or to "reach back" and grant his application for permission to appeal denied over a decade ago. Mr. Johnson has presented no legal basis for denying the State's Motion to Set Execution Date. Therefore, the State's motion to Set Execution Date is GRANTED. It is hereby ORDERED, ADJUDGED and DECREED by this Court that the Warden of the Riverbend Maximum Security Institution, or his designee shall execute the sentence of death as provided by law on the 2nd day of December, 2009, unless otherwise ordered by this Court or other appropriate authority. Counsel for Cecil C. Johnson, Jr., shall provide a copy of any order staying execution of this order to the Office of the Clerk of the Appellate Court in Nashville. The Clerk shall expeditiously furnish a copy of any order of stay to the Warden of the Riverbend Maximum Security Institution.

IT IS SO ORDERED. PER CURIAM

Chapter Ten

1. "Will Tennessee Fix Its Death Penalty?" by William Redick, *Tennessee Bar Journal,* September 2009, https://www.tba.org/?pg=Articles&blAction =showEntry&blogEntry=9314. Copyright Tennessee Bar Association; used with permission.

2. *Id.* Specifically, the ABA's 93 recommendations addressed problems in need of reform in the following areas that impact the administration of the death penalty in Tennessee: (1) the collection, preservation, and testing of DNA and other types of evidence; (2) law enforcement identifications and interrogations; (3) crime laboratories and medical examiner offices; (4) prosecutorial professionalism; (5) defense services; (6) the direct appeal process; (7) the state post-conviction process; (8) clemency; (9) capital jury instructions; (10) judicial independence; (11) racial and ethnic minorities; (12) mental retardation and mental illness.

3. "An Odd Combination," by Suzanne Craig Robertson, September 2009, *Tennessee Bar Journal,* https://www.tba.org/?pg=Articles&blAction =showEntry&blogEntry=9315. Copyright Tennessee Bar Association; used with permission.

Chapter Eleven

1. "Judge Refuses to Stop Johnson Execution," by Lucas L. Johnson II, *Legal News,* Dec. 1, 2009, http://www.legalnews.com/detroit/589470; *Johnson v. Bredesen,* Case No. 3:09-1133 (M.D. Tenn. Nov. 30, 2009), https://casetext. com/case/johnson-v-bredesen-2.

2. Sarah Ann Johnson, for Herself and on Behalf of the Late Cecil Johnson v. Dr. Bruce Levy, http://www.tncourts.gov/sites/default/files/order _of_the_coa_re_motion_of_dr._levy_for_emergency_stay.pdf.

Chapter Twelve

1. "Cecil C. Johnson execution," by Kate Howard, *The Tennessean*, Dec. 1, 2009 (updated 5:57 p.m.). Copyright *USA Today* Network/*The Tennessean*; used with permission.

Chapter Thirteen

1. *Cecil C. Johnson Jr. v. Ricky Bell, Warden*, U.S. Court of Appeals for the 6th Circuit, filed April 29, 2008. Appeal from the United States District Court for the Middle District of Tennessee at Nashville, No. 99-00047—Robert L. Echols, District Judge; Before BATCHELDER, COLE and GIBBONS, Circuit Judges at http://www.ca6.uscourts.gov/opinions.pdf/08a0167p-06.pdf.

2. Read an overview of Cecil's legal journey, including witnesses at trial, at the Tennesseans for Alternatives to the Death Penalty website, "Tennessee Executes Cecil Johnson," Dec. 3, 2009, https://tennesseedeathpenalty.org/tennessee-executes-cecil-johnson.

3. "Faces of Justice: Justices E. Riley Anderson and Adolpho A. Birch Jr. Leave the Tennessee Supreme Court," by Julie Swearingen, August 2006 *Tennessee Bar Journal*, https://www.tba.org/docDownload/2016619. Copyright Tennessee Bar Association; used with permission.

4. *Id.*

5. "The Trial of Cecil Johnson," by Donald F. Paine, February 2010 *Tennessee Bar Journal*, https://www.tba.org/docDownload/2016620. Copyright Tennessee Bar Association; used with permission. Paine quotes the juror as published in 632 S.W.2d at 549. The case is *State v. Johnson*, 632 S.W.2d 542 (Tenn., 1982).

6. *State v. Johnson*, 632 S.W.2d 542 (Tenn., 1982). Also, *Johnson v. State*, 797 S.W.2d 578 (1990), Supreme Court of Tennessee, at Nashville, http://law.justia.com/cases/tennessee/supreme-court/1990/797-s-w-2d-578-2.html. The Court at that time were Justices William H. D. Fones, Robert Cooper Sr., William Harbison, Charles O'Brien (who wrote the opinion) and Frank Drowota, who was chief justice. Justices Fones, Cooper, and Harbison concurred with the opinion, and Justice Drowota filed a separate concurring opinion.

Chapter Fourteen

1. *Cecil C. Johnson v. Phil Bredesen, Governor of the State of Tennessee; George M. Little, Commissioner of the Tennessee Department of Corrections; and Ricky Bell, Warden Riverbend Maximum Security Institution, in their official capacities, Defendants,* Dec. 1, 2009, https://cases.justia.com/federal/district-courts/tennessee/tnmdce/3:2009cv01133/46373/17/0.pdf?ts=13771 45343. This document outlines the steps in the case.

2. "Justices spar over Tennessee execution," by Bill Mears, *CNN News,* Dec. 2, 2009, 2:24 p.m. EST.

3. *Id.*

4. *Cecil C. Johnson Jr. v. Ricky Bell, Warden,* U.S. Court of Appeals for the 6th Circuit, filed April 29, 2008, at http://www.ca6.uscourts.gov/opinions.pdf/08a0167p-06.pdf. "As for the other three witnesses, the State admits that the prosecution withheld evidence that would have impeached each witness' identification of Johnson as the perpetrator. ... Johnson's case is not even a close one."

5. "Justices spar over Tennessee execution," by Bill Mears, *CNN News,* Dec. 2, 2009, 2:24 p.m. EST.

Chapter Fifteen

1. Erik Schelzig, *Knoxville News Sentinel,* Dec. 2, 2009. (It's unclear who the "two brothers" were. We were only aware of his younger brother, David Johnson, being there.) Copyright Associated Press; used with permission.

2. "Cecil C. Johnson execution," by Kate Howard, *The Tennessean,* Dec. 1, 2009. Copyright *USA Today* Network/*The Tennessean*; used with permission.

3. *Id.*

4. Tennessee executes Cecil Johnson," by Chris Echegaray, *The Tennessean,* Dec. 2, 2009. Copyright *USA Today* Network/*The Tennessean*; used with permission.

Chapter Seventeen

1. "Judge to decide on autopsy for executed killer," by Clay Carey and Chris Echegaray, *The Tennessean,* Dec. 3, 2009. Copyright *USA Today* Network/*The Tennessean*; used with permission.

2. "The Death Penalty in Black and White: Who Lives, Who Dies, Who Decides," by Richard C. Dieter, The Death Penalty Information Center, June 1998, https://deathpenaltyinfo.org/death-penalty-black-and-white-who-lives -who-dies-who-decides.

3. "North Carolina Man Executed in Deaths of 3 Police Officers," *The New York Times,* March 16, 1984, http://www.nytimes.com/1984/03/16/us /north-carolina-man-executed-in-deaths-of-3-police-officers.html.

4. "Facing Controversy: Struggling with Capital Punishment in North Carolina," University of North Carolina libraries, http://exhibits.lib.unc .edu/exhibits/show/capital-punishment/biographies/barfield.

5. *Gregg v. Georgia,* 428 U.S. 153 (1976), https://supreme.justia.com /cases/federal/us/428/153. The issue was whether the death penalty was unconstitutional per se under the Eighth Amendment as cruel and unusual punishment. The court said it was not. This came four years after the Court's 1972 decision in *Furman v. Georgia,* that the application of the death penalty was unconstitutional. But in 1976, *Gregg* reinstated the death penalty.

Chapter Eighteen

1. *State v. Johnson,* 632 S.W.2d 542 (Tenn. 1982).

2. "Cecil C. Johnson execution," by Kate Howard, *The Tennessean,* Dec. 1, 2009 (updated 5:57 p.m.). Copyright *USA Today* Network/*The Tennessean*; used with permission.

3. *Id.*

4. *Johnson v. Bell,* page 6, 21, U.S. Court of Appeals for the 6th Circuit, filed April 29, 2008, at http://www.ca6.uscourts.gov/opinions .pdf/08a0167p-06.pdf.

5. "Cecil C. Johnson execution," by Kate Howard, *The Tennessean,* Dec. 1, 2009. Copyright *USA Today* Network/*The Tennessean*; used with permission.

6. *Id.*

7. *Johnson v. Bell,* U.S. Court of Appeals for the 6th Circuit, filed April 29, 2008, at http://www.ca6.uscourts.gov/opinions.pdf/08a0167p-06.pdf.

8. *Id.* "The entire case against Johnson consisted of only four witnesses and no physical evidence. One of the four witnesses was originally scheduled as an alibi witness to corroborate Johnson's innocence. On the day before trial, after a coerced midnight encounter with the State prosecutor,

that witness flipped. As for the other three witnesses, the State admits that the prosecution withheld evidence that would have impeached each witness' identification of Johnson as the perpetrator. ... Johnson's case is not even a close one. As in *Kyles, Brigano,* and others, the same is true here: confidence that Johnson's verdict would have been the same simply cannot survive a recap of the suppressed evidence and its significance for the prosecution. The withheld evidence, taken together, reveals at a minimum that one witness's first and most lucid description of the assailant did not comport with his in-court identification, that one witness may not have [been in the] store on the night of the crimes, and that one witness implicated someone other than Johnson when confronted with a photo array containing Johnson's picture. These were the same three witnesses that the Supreme Court of Tennessee called Johnson's "insurmountable problem." *Johnson,* 632 S.W.2d at 547. Had the prosecution disclosed the six items of withheld evidence, competent defense counsel may very well have destroyed the value of their identifications, or at least raised serious questions in the jurors' minds as to their reliability. This is to say nothing of the potential inferences of police and prosecutorial misconduct that the jurors may also rationally have made had they been apprised of the suppressed evidence. Simply put, Johnson's defense was substantially crippled in cross-examining the three critical witnesses on the only serious issue in this case—identification."

9. *Id.* [See *Lindsey,* 769 F.2d at 1040. "No reasonable court can have confidence in the decision of a jury that did not hear this withheld evidence." *Castleberry,* 349 F.3d at 294 (citation omitted).]

10. *Id.,* note 20, page 19.

Chapter Nineteen

1. Letter from Hal Hardin to James G. Thomas, Nov. 16, 2009, provided to the author by Mr. Hardin, and used with permission.

2. *Id.* Here is the partial text of Hal Hardin's letter:

Regarding the facts at hand, the following questions have to be answered:

1. **Was there exculpatory evidence that the defense did not have during the trial of this case?** The answer to that question is: "Yes."

2. **Did the defense attorney make a request for exculpatory evidence?** Again, the answer is yes.

3. **Was the exculpatory evidence material?** Would it most probably affect the outcome of a trial? Yes. It is doubtful to believe that any honest experienced trial lawyer would doubt that.

Eye witness identification, contrary to popular belief, is some of the weakest evidence one can have at trial. That fact has been established by the Courts and researched extensively. The damning evidence in this case was the eye witness identification of witnesses. If the jury had known that these two witnesses had given conflicting statements, indeed contradictory statements, one would have to conclude that a good, law-abiding juror would give great weight to the conflicting statements. This would be especially true since the contradictory statements by the eye witnesses were made immediately after the crime than their later statements. Such contemporary statements are known to be much more valuable than statements made at later dates.

4. **Where was the exculpatory evidence found?** It was found in the prosecutor's own file. While the good faith or the bad faith of a prosecutor in failing to turn over exculpatory evidence is normally not a controlling issue, denial of due process is the same regardless of a prosecutor's good faith or lack thereof. Occasionally, police officers fail to turn over statements to the prosecutor. However, this is no excuse. It is the ethical and legal duty of a prosecutor to look through his or her own file and also the file of all agents who were involved in the case. In this case, the exculpatory evidence that should have been turned over was found in the District Attorney's own file. One would have to conclusively assume that any District Attorney would go through his or her own file prior to the trying of the lawsuit, especially this high profile lawsuit. I believe that the second and third chair prosecutors most probably did not go through every paper. The lead prosecutor most certainly would have done that.

5. **Was the evidence material?** It is my understanding that the State in essence has stipulated that the evidence is exculpatory. I do not see how anyone could argue the materiality of the withheld evidence.

6. **Has any jury seen this evidence?** Obviously not.

After a cursory review, I believe that the above reflects the law regarding exculpatory evidence and specifically as it applies to the facts in this case.

3. *Id.* See also *Johnson v. Bell*, page 19, U.S. Court of Appeals for the 6th Circuit, filed April 29, 2008, at http://www.ca6.uscourts.gov/opinions.pdf/08a0167p-06.pdf.

4. *Id., Johnson v. Bell.*

5. *The Rooker Report,* a publication of the Davidson County, Tenn., Circuit Court Clerk's Office, April 2011, https://circuitclerk.nashville.gov/wp-content/uploads/rr2011_04.pdf.

6. Belmont University College of Law faculty page for Torry Johnson, http://www.belmont.edu/law/facultyadmin/faculty-torry-johnson.html.

7. Email from Victor "Torry" Johnson to the author, June 8, 2015, and used with permission.

8. *Johnson v. Bell*, page 19, U.S. Court of Appeals for the 6th Circuit, filed April 29, 2008, at http://www.ca6.uscourts.gov/opinions.pdf/08a0167p-06.pdf.

9. Email from Victor "Torry" Johnson to the author, June 8, 2015, and used with permission.

10. "Cecil C. Johnson execution," by Kate Howard, *The Tennessean,* Dec. 1, 2009 (updated 5:57 p.m.). Copyright *USA Today* Network/*The Tennessean*; used with permission.

Chapter Twenty

1. Death Penalty Information Center, "Facts About the Death Penalty: Recent Studies on Race," updated June 24, 2022, https://documents.deathpenaltyinfo.org/pdf/FactSheet.pdf.

2. "Tennessee's Death Penalty Lottery," by Bradley A. MacLean and H.E. Miller Jr., *Tennessee Journal of Law and Policy*, Summer 2018, Vol. 13, Issue 1, page 85. Mr. Miller surveyed Tennessee's first-degree murder cases from 1977 through 2018 and found that the death penalty is carried out in an arbitrary manner. In this article, MacLean and Miller examined the arbitrariness of the system, including "infrequency of application, geographical disparity, timing and natural deaths, error rates, quality of defense representation, prosecutorial discretion and misconduct, defendants' impairments, race, and judicial disparity."

3. *Furman v. Georgia*, 408 U.S. at 306 (1972) determined that the death penalty constituted cruel and unusual punishment, in violation of the Eighth and Fourteenth Amendments. However, in 1976, *Gregg v. Georgia* upheld the legality of the death penalty.

ABOUT THE AUTHOR

SUZANNE CRAIG ROBERTSON HAS SERVED AS THE DIRECTOR OF communications of the Tennessee Bar Association and is a former editor of the *Tennessee Bar Journal*, where, for more than three decades, she interviewed and wrote about state supreme court justices, recovering addicts, lawyer-missionaries, low-income people in need of legal services, trailblazing women, the legal system, and more. A lifelong Christian who has questioned her churches many times but never her faith, she is a graduate of the University of Tennessee and has a Master of Arts from the Nasland-Mann School of Creative and Professional Writing at Spalding University. A mother and grandmother, she lives with her husband in Nashville, Tennessee, twenty minutes and worlds away from Riverbend Maximum Security Institution.